About the Author

Lucy Rose began her transition in her early twenties while at university, later graduating with a BSc in physics with astronomy and an MA in creative writing, and now lives as a woman in Southampton, England. She has written for various magazines and websites, often on the topic of the transgender experience, and is now the lead guitarist in the transgender-queer rock band Hunting Hearts.

By My Name

Lucy Rose

By My Name

Vanguard Press

VANGUARD PAPERBACK

© Copyright 2024
Lucy Rose

The right of Lucy Rose to be identified as author of this work has been asserted by her in accordance with the Copyright, Designs and Patents Act 1988.

All Rights Reserved

No reproduction, copy or transmission of this publication may be made without written permission.
No paragraph of this publication may be reproduced, copied or transmitted save with the written permission of the publisher, or in accordance with the provisions of the Copyright Act 1956 (as amended).

Any person who commits any unauthorised act in relation to this publication may be liable to criminal prosecution and civil claims for damages.

A CIP catalogue record for this title is available from the British Library.

ISBN 978 1 80016 781 0

*Vanguard Press is an imprint of
Pegasus Elliot Mackenzie Publishers Ltd.*
www.pegasuspublishers.com

First Published in 2024

**Vanguard Press
Sheraton House Castle Park
Cambridge England**
Printed & Bound in Great Britain

To Olly.

Acknowledgements

By its very nature, the transition is an intensely personal journey, and writing about it is even more so. That being said, there are several people I would like to acknowledge for the part they have played in this chapter of my life. First and foremost would be my parents, who, even though they found it difficult at first, came around in the end and supported me every step of the way. I would also like to call out the members of the various theatrical societies with whom I performed during my university career, and who gave me an infinite space to experiment with who I was and how I wanted to identify as I was just starting to contemplate my gender identity. Then there are my fellow bandmates in Hunting Hearts, who have not only been compatriots in the struggle for self-definition, but have picked me up when I was down and given me a voice to help others in the community so they might not feel as alone as I did. To this end, I also want to thank the team at Pegasus for taking a chance on an admittedly unconventional book and controversial topic, allowing me to reach even more in need of advice and help during these uncertain times for the LGBT+ community. And lastly, I want to thank my partners for more than I could ever adequately put here, but for, in short, giving me the chance to experience more of life than I thought I would ever get the chance to.

Prologue

Memory is a funny thing. It becomes sun-bleached over time, to the point of being almost unrecognisable. If it was not for my desire to write this book, this account of my transition, I doubt I would have remembered much of it at all. It is a journey defined by the slow accumulation of subtle moments. Few are notable on their own but together they construct the prospect of years, which has resulted for me in a far better future than I otherwise would have had. And I believe that with all my heart.

But while it may be difficult to describe the transition as a whole, it is even harder to pinpoint where it began. For my doctors, they would look to when I changed my name in the summer of 2017. Or you might say it was when I came out to my family before that. Or when I sought a referral to the gender identity clinic in the autumn of 2015. Or when I came out to my friends, or to myself, or when I was unknowingly envious of the girls around me during my academic career as a teenager.

Either way, whichever definition you choose, the truth is inescapable: the transition was a foregone conclusion. It was simply a matter of time before it happened. It could never have gone any other way. I was bound for this course the moment I was born. This is the 'me' I was always supposed to have been, and the road was longer than necessary simply because I was a little slow in realising that. And each person along that road – friends, family, and professionals – were allies in that endeavour. Without them, I might still not know and be trudging on as before, discontent yet unaware of why I feel that 'splinter in my mind'.

And as I now come to the end of my own personal journey, I wanted to catalogue it as best I could. I did not do this only for my own sense of closure and completeness, but to unveil its secrets and dispel its taboos.

I have confined eight years to these pages because the transition should not be shrouded in mystery, with each new transgender person forced to discover it for themselves against a field of ignorance and opposition. It should be freely available to learn from, improve upon, and to use in one's own quest for liberation. And it should not be for those around them to go through it alone or unaware. They, too, should have access to the material they need to understand what their loved one is undergoing so they can adjust to this change and help all reach a positive endpoint.

When I started my own journey, dressing up in secret in my room after my parents had gone to bed, pacing the two spare steps to try and figure out the walk, I would have found such information invaluable. While I am sure the facts and forums were out there, they were not as easily accessible as they are today and the understanding had not reached the same level as it has now.

My first understanding of the transition was as a single operation, as shown in media, with the 'sex change operation' often being used as a joke or plot point in various shows and programmes. This is not helped by major celebrity figures who undergo the transition in record time due to their resources and access to private and personalised healthcare.

For most people, myself included, this is not how it goes. It is a long, frustrating, and confusing ordeal, a front-loaded process where years churn and a person is reforged beneath the surface before the first doctor is ever seen, and much of it one has to figure out for themselves. There are, of course, elements to anyone's transition that are wholly unique, being as many stories as there are transgender people to tell them, and I can only speak from my lone viewpoint as someone assigned male at birth, but there are some common facets I will try to explain and illuminate through this book.

My hope is that those who are considering the transition can read this and know they are not alone, and that what they are feeling is normal. I want to help educate not only the emotional side but also the administrative, and the personal steps the transition can require. It will not be a complete guide. It never could be. But it could be a springboard from which one could leap into their own version of the transition with all the information they need to make the best of it they can.

And for their loved ones, friends and family, this can be a window into their mind, how to help, what actions to take, what to expect and how to reconcile the past with this new normal. The transition is for those around the individual as well, and they, too, will need time and support to reach an equilibrium.

To get there, however, I must issue a warning of sorts for the contents of this book. For any reader about to embark, please be aware of the personal and intimate nature of much of what is about to be discussed, be it emotional, psychological or physical. It comes with the territory, I am afraid, and there is no way to talk about the transition without bringing up what is normally so closely guarded about a person.

So, during the course of this, I will be speaking about personal medical details, parts of my anatomy that are relevant to the discussion, and the impact on my mental health during the various stages of the journey. This is all stuff I have worked through and may be triggering or uncomfortable to some people, but it is important to note that these are normal parts of life in the transition, and the more they are spoken the less taboo or mysterious they become. Hopefully, then, they will be easier to address and overcome for those going through the transition and for those around them. Ideally, a conversation can then be had constructively, with understanding and the aim of healing in mind.

And to draw the material I needed for this, I turned to a series of blog posts I wrote throughout the transition. I linked them together, bulked them up with the benefit of hindsight, and used my experience to collate them into a single narrative. The blogs themselves were snapshots into individual aspects of the transition, but it was my aim to use them to create something larger, a cohesive whole that covers as much of my transition as I can reasonably describe lending aid where possible.

Thus, I am writing these several years after the fact and for that reason, many of the smaller details may have been lost or forgotten. The transition is such a long process that it is impossible to recount everything or give every instance its due weight. These blogs written close to or at the time should help, but I am sure there were things that did not make it into these short-form pieces of writing. But had it not been for them, I imagine much of the transition would have become an amorphous jumble of confused memories, a haze of change and struggle, of smiles and discovery. In a way, it still is, but these islands of recollection give me points around which to focus.

It is the same as with any large, impactful event, be it traumatic or euphoric – or a bizarre mixture of both. The mind becomes selective about what it can or wants to remember. For example, I had just come out of a period of serious illness that nearly drove me to the edge – I will go into this in more detail later as it does play a part in the transition towards the end – but there are two months during the worst of it that I simply cannot remember. My mind has blocked it out as if to protect me. Perhaps it is doing something similar with the transition, but instead of protecting me from pain, maybe it is saying that this chapter is now over. Stop dwelling on it and move on. It is finally time, after eight years, to live the life for which you have worked so hard.

Stop thinking.

Start living.

And I will.

I promise.

But first, this is where I, as present Lucy, leave you in the hands of an augmented past Lucy to start the story of my transition as best and as clearly as I can. I hope this proves useful to you, reader, and that these few halting words do little in their effort to stop the tide of ignorance and prejudice against the transgender community. If all we can do is put a bit of good into the world, even if it might seem hopeless, even if it is in the form of only a mildly interesting tale, then that is what I will do. Because each drop comes together, in time, to make an ocean of its own. Enough, perhaps, to make a change.

Part One

Transgendered Substantiation
The Social Transition

Chapter One

But How Do You Know?

The assumption of heterosexuality and that you are the gender you were assigned at birth is so ingrained into the fabric of social discourse, and especially when it comes to raising a child, that for nearly twenty years I believed I was straight and a man. It turns out I was misinformed.

But going from one to the other is a leap that eludes reason at first. I grew up as an outsider, among my school cohort, among my friends and, to an extent, among my own family. I thought this was because I was inherently unlikeable. The reason I felt out of place was that it was my fault I did not fit in. I was a teacher's pet and a tryhard because this loneliness and our own familial unrest, which I will not go into here, meant the only acceptance I found was through excelling, by being the unfeeling, always perfect rock. I was the one that could bring home good news on bad days and receive praise when no one else would otherwise look at me twice.

This has become so deeply a part of me that it lives on in me today, despite having identified it and come to understand its roots. It has caused an overwhelming fear of loneliness and inadequacy, the thought the reason people are not with me is that I am not good enough. How then was I supposed to know that there was not something wrong with me, but instead that there was not something right?

It was not that I was not good enough, it was that I was not all there in the first place. Of course I could not be accepted fully if there was not a full person to accept. Yet how are you supposed to know what the problem is? How can you discover that it is your gender identity that is the cause of all these difficulties? And even if you do, how are you meant to know if this is the truth or if the issue lies elsewhere?

This is not helped by the general lack of visibility for transgender people in society and in media. Away from very strictly defined areas of society or the internet, there is no real conversation around transgender people, and when there is it is often harmful and nearly always distorted and confusing.

So why was I alone? Why did people not seem to like me? Why was I always awkward and shy? Why was I envious of the girls in my year? Was this just normal teenage angst or was there something more? No one had spoken to me about the changes of this period outside the usual lessons at school, which themselves omit anything not already chained to the binary. The subtle mental struggles, the steady awakening of one's personality. All this was supplanted by 'hair will grow in places it did not before' and other such surface-level features.

So why, when I did finally reach something resembling an answer, how was I supposed to know for sure?

This is the question I was either asked the most or the one I asked myself the most, and it is frustratingly impossible to answer by anything resembling logic. I can only talk about the emotions of the puzzle.

I came to understand that I might be transgender through a linear fashion, a series of events that led from one to the other, in a progression that, in hindsight, suited my scientific brain, being a physicist and a pragmatist at heart.

It started in my second year at university. You could say I had been questioning for a while at that point, meandering my way through the spectrum, unsure of where I fit in. Was I bisexual? Was I gay? I decided to join the LGBT+ society at my university to find others like me. I wanted to talk things through and hopefully understand what was going on a little more. For those for whom this is not possible, it might be an alternative to see if there are online forums or local support groups or charities you can join.

In this society, I met members from all over the spectrum, including transgender individuals. They offered me, without any cost to them, one of the most important things that any questioning individual can be given – they gave me a space free from judgement in which I could experiment further. I could play out all different combinations to see which one stuck until I finally felt at home in my body and around my friends.

When I started with the society, I thought I was a gay man, but as time went on, I found I wanted to present and be identified as female on occasion. I mainly kept this to my bedroom or the occasional night out. I did not want it to interfere with my day-to-day life too much, and I was terrified of these two worlds colliding, of members of the LGBT+ society meeting those from the theatrical societies of which I was a part, as though this would be the end of my own personal world and would force me into some limelight before I was ready.

This did happen, in a way, but it was at a time of my choosing, though I will get to that later. First, I want to double back and understand where and why I started wanting to dress. During a holiday, I took up a week's work experience in London for a science magazine. It was paid, though not much, but for a student, even £100 was a considerable sum. At the end of that week, with this money in my pocket, I walked past a clothes store and saw the models pictured in its window.

That old envy, which at that time was an undefined feeling that nonetheless wormed its way into my mind, was stoked and I found myself inside the shop without really knowing why. I bought myself some lingerie with the money I had earned, awkwardly dealing at checkout before rushing back home confused about what I had done and why. I am still not sure what drove me at that moment, but it began, in its own way, a period of reflection and discovery.

Earlier, I mentioned that I was a scientist when it came down to it and this is where that mindset really came to the fore. Late at night, alone in my room at home, I dressed up in front of my mirror and felt the first stirrings of something. I actually liked what I was seeing. After the puberty through which I had suffered and the scars with which it had left me, to like part of what I saw in the mirror was novel and exhilarating. Though, at that point, I could not tell whether this was anything more than a sexual thrill, but it nonetheless pushed me to understand more.

So I continued.

I ordered more online and bought a wig, a long auburn number, and once again that feeling was there. The more pieces I added, the stronger it became. I then turned to the internet to see if I could find out what this all was and if it had a name. My exposure to the transgender community and its terminology was limited to the few conversations I had had at university and its clearly misrepresented counterpart in the media.

But while I was doing my research, I came upon the umbrella term 'transgender' and the others that existed under its definition. I will outline these in more detail later, but for now, they were a light bulb that let me know there was a direction to take, that what I was experiencing was okay and something other people also felt.

So I continued.

I tested out the lower rungs of the transgender ladder first, then up to see if I found my place. I went through experiment-conclusion, experiment-conclusion and at each stage analysed how it made me feel. And the feeling of something being indescribably 'right' was there with me each step of the way, leading me on, a want to find out where it would go and how it would end up. It felt… good. I had not felt good about myself… perhaps ever, so I chased the sensation, an elusive promise of happiness and something better. Something different from the person I was.

So I continued.

It did feel strange, scary and in a way shameful, this secret conclave, as though there was some lie inherent in the act. I did not know whether with this I was fooling myself, as well as those around me, or whether I had always been the fool. Would my unmasking only cause greater pain for those who knew me? Did I need this to be happy?

There was a lingering, unsaid threat to my established order that part of me wanted to avoid. I wanted to go back to when things were easy. I felt like an impostor doing it for kicks. A simple cry for attention. A desire for the enforced, sterile pragmatist to actually feel something.

Or was it more?

Whatever happened, I knew it was going to hurt.

But I continued because I had to.

For anyone else going through this stage of discovery, I urge you to not feel shame or disgust for being different or having to hide yourself away at society's behest. It is just part of the journey. And I wanted to see it through. I wanted to know who I was and where this was taking me. In the end, it led me to get the shape through tucking and breast-forms. When added to the wig, this was where something clicked, and it was a kind of release.

I had a way out.

But how to show myself? I was unfinished but I had reached the end of what my current experiments would allow. I needed to come out, at least only to friends to start with. I will cover this more in its own dedicated chapter, but I picked the night and measured myself for it. A drag night. A pub crawl with those who as of yet did not know.

The context of the night broke the ice, established the image and the possibility, and allowed me the chance to basically say: "Ta-Da! This is me now!"

Thankfully, they were all accepting and I need not have worried. They offered me the same space as the LGBT+ society, that infinite ground to test and try, to fail and remake, to support and guide until I was ready to stand on my own two feet and walk the further paths of this journey. These roads I will leave for later, but rest assured – I continued.

Because through my entire young life, I had felt like I was playing the part that was expected of me and hid everything else behind the walls of some great fortress. But the battlements were ripped apart, stone by stone. I had to abandon what I had previously dictated as safe and risk everything on leap after leap, trial after trial. I was terrified. Terrified of taking the next one. Terrified that this feeling would fade between those few nights I could present as female. Terrified that all this would leave me worse than when I had started. Terrified that even though I had not liked the person I was, at least I had found some form of acceptance in the even subtler social performance I had mastered in my youth. I was not popular by any means, but in the wasteland of school I had a few close friends and academic recognition, and in the turmoil of my family I had the role of the emotional rock, the perfect child who could always bring home good news to earn attention and respect.

These were all the coverings of a deep-seated loneliness that, even as I write this, has not fully left, but did I want to risk what little I had found? After all, where was I going? There are many different terms and definitions, almost as many as there are people to experience them. While I am not one to put labels on anyone, it did help to have a starting point that I could look to and say: "That is me… kind of." Yet, was this enough to go on? Could a doubt and a wish be the basis of a brand-new life?

To this end, I will put below how I understand some of the broader terms, where I fit in and how that image has changed over time. However, I also encourage you to research further.

Cisgender (often abbreviated to 'cis'): This means you identify as the gender you were assigned at birth (e.g. cisgender man, cis woman).

Transgender: This means you do not identify as the gender you were assigned at birth. Transgender can be a specific identity, meaning you are the opposite gender to that assigned at birth (trans man/trans woman), but it can also be used as a catch-all term meaning anyone who is not cisgender, regardless of whether their gender is binary or not.

Non-binary: non-binary is another umbrella term that includes anyone whose gender is not binary (i.e. not just male or female). It can also be used as an identity in itself, meaning someone who identifies outside the male/female binary, or as having no gender. This can include third gender, intersex, genderfluid or agender individuals.

These are quite quick-cut labels and will not perfectly describe everyone. This is all a spectrum, somewhere on which we all exist to unique degrees, so to quote a rather friendly pirate: 'they are more like guidelines'. And as guidelines tend to do, they are constantly evolving alongside the social understanding of gender. Two main changes I have seen over the years are the disuse of the term 'transexual' and the other is a movement to promote gender neutrality, to use gender-neutral pronouns and terminology and to end discrimination against gender altogether. After all, gender is, in a way, really just a social construct based upon the false equivalence with one's biological sex.

And while some may experience a kind of an awakening when it comes to self-discovery, for me it was more a creeping doubt that something was not right in what I had previously known. The fastidious identity I had crafted for myself over twenty-something years, where I was the conscientious worker, the good student, the robust child, was lacking. I could not fully express all that I believed I was.

This brings me to the point where I fully knew that I was transgender and wanted to go through with the complete transition process. I realised that everything I had known before was simply a method of presenting what I thought people wanted to see. I was not my own person. I was their image and the only acceptance I had found was by meeting that image.

So, as a final test, I decided to act in a show where I was a male character who needed to have a beard. For three months I grew a beard. I intentionally trapped myself in the stereotypical male mould. I lived that image. I existed as that expectation with the newfound knowledge I had acquired. I went back to how it used to be to see if it was any better or worse than I remembered. Did I still need it? Could I do without it?

And I hated every second of it!

Even though I got to perform at the Edinburgh Fringe for my trouble, I wanted to dig the skin from my skull with a carving knife to get that thing off my face. That feeling of being locked into a role I knew was wrong was what woke me up and let me know that this was the path forward. Transitioning was not about becoming someone new.

It was about being me: unleashed.

Chapter Two

Coming Out

Acceptance first comes from within. It took me a while to accept myself as who I was becoming. For many years after, I remember feeling some element of regret, of wanting things to go back to when they were simple and easy. But before coming out to everyone, I first had to come out to myself, and it took a while. There were always doubts of whether this would last, fears over what opposition and struggles I would face as a result, and a certain reticence to commit to a completely new image and style of living and all the consequences that entailed, both personal and social. But once I had, I knew there was no going back.

Whenever I had the chance to present as a female in those early days, such as for a night out, I would be terrified that when I put on the dress and did my make-up I would no longer feel the same buzz I once did. I was scared I would be emptier for the time that had passed between disparate chances. But when I did, there was always that relief when I looked in the mirror and knew it was all still true. This was me. For all its trials, this was me.

For all that can lie on the other side of this divide, to admit it to yourself and then expose it to others was the hardest part of the journey so far. Until now, it had all been self-contained; there was an escape if necessary, a way to go back and pretend it had never happened. It could have been a phase, a gimmick for social theatrics, nothing that would change life permanently and uncertainly. I had my daylight image and the recognition, albeit vicarious, it had given me.

But this was where I had to put myself out there and have others hold up this new view of myself against what they had always known. I had to abandon the safety of my chiselled cave, formed from the expectations I had so far spent my life meeting, to the detriment of my own identity, and I did not know if I was ready. I did not know if I was strong enough to survive this inquisition. I was afraid that if I left it alone, these feelings would eventually fade, and I would go right back to where I started. A person fashioned from the coattails and second-hand glances of their peers, and nothing else besides.

But how do you come out?

There is no single answer to that question. It really depends on your personal situation and the context of your family and friends. I grew up in the theatre. From a young age, I was on stage and among performers, singers, and actors. For as long as I can remember, the wings and boards of an auditorium were my home. And the stereotype of that world is pretty much true enough. It is a very LGBT+-friendly environment. And while I was terrified at first of my multiple lives colliding, when I resolved to make the leap, to consolidate myself, coming out to those friends who were not part of my LGBT+ circle was accepted without issue and I could go on from there. As I mentioned before, I chose a drag pub crawl, let them get used to it, and basically said they were stuck with me like that from now on. No complaints, on we move and there you go.

But of the friends I left behind before university, it took years for me to reconnect.

It goes back to self-identity. It was as a male that they knew me, and I did not know how they would react. The dynamic would shift. How could I be anyone else but who they had always known? That person had been somewhat of an outcast in every circle, this one included, to an extent. Once again, I had found acceptance in the role I played. If I disrupted that, then what else would I have? But in that same vein, I did not want to revert to how I had fit into their group now that I had uncovered these previously unknown parts of me. How would they contend with such ingrained routines? Maybe I preferred to remember the good times we used to have and leave it at that, rather than risk it all now in retrospect.

This is doubly true for family. The risk only grows with the amount of time spent together before the big day.

Coming out to family was the hardest for me. It may be that you have accepting parents, siblings, and extended family members, but it is quite common for the older generations to be more conservative in nature. For me, I came out in stages. I spent a while meandering through the spectrum, at first I was bisexual, then gay, then a transvestite. This last point I said on a holiday, which promptly brought festivities to a stop and caused several uncomfortable dinners and conversations. It was even recommended that I seek therapy to talk it through with someone.

I did.

They concluded I did not need therapy. My family did.

But when it came to saying I was transgender and wanted to go through the transition, I did this via a handwritten letter to my parents and then let them spread the news how they wished. In this, I also included my aims, the route I would take, the timeline, the risks and the consequences, as far as I knew them at the time. I wanted them to have the fullest picture possible so it was not an unknown or anything scary. I also wanted them to know that I was serious, that this was not a whim, but researched and considered what I truly desired to do.

In the end, I chose a letter because I did not want to leave it impersonal, such as in a text or e-mail, but could not face doing it in person. A letter, then, was the compromise.

How and when you do it is up to you and I wish you the best of luck. I will say, however, that you will experience backlash and doubt, the 'it's just a phase' line, and any other number of excuses to make it not real. I know I encountered all these and more even in my generally liberal and loving family. And you will have to once more face the wall.

Doubt.

In the days running up to 'the moment,' I questioned myself endlessly over whether this was right for me, whether I should burden those around me with this knowledge, and I wondered whether I was strong enough to stand up to their probes and the inevitable tides of change. I fell upon the shame of the lie. Either way, I was a deceiver. A son in the act; a daughter they had never truly known.

But in the end, their words were not my validation.

This was not a plea for help, a cry for attention, or even self-ratification. It was a statement of intent. This was who I am. This was how I could best invest myself in the world. How could I be of impact when I was not a full person myself? I must unite my internal identity with my outward perception to overcome this dysphoria and become a person worthy of action. My memory of deceit was merely my evolution. Because I had come this far. I had passed every test I had set for myself. I was the sum of all that had led me here.

Instead of melting into the background as I have for most of my life, I had the flexibility to track how I might change, and now aware of the fallacy of a single, permanent identity there came the desire to step outside my sanctuary and seek change. I could experience all life has to offer. And I wanted it! I had already missed out on so much playing the part of duty. I wanted to go places I had never been, do things I had never done, and meet people and make friends I might never have met. How could I be ashamed of that?

All this informs who I am and whatever pinnacle I reach, not the lonely fortress I was scared to leave. For that reason, I was more terrified now of staying the same. Normality is frightening for the loss of potential implied in another decade of the quotidian performance. And while the transition process does involve a lot of waiting around, it is nothing compared to what I had before. I know what it is like for the years to pass with nought but accreditation to show for it. All I needed was the room to explore and be sure of myself and support for whatever came next. But I will not lie, this is a challenge, not just for you, but for those who love you. Though I will expand my thoughts on this in a future chapter.

Before I turn to more administrative matters, I want to discuss something that is rarely talked about when this topic is broached. You will never come out only one time. Each new friend, each new relationship, each new job, and even each new service contact is tinged with the knowledge that they do not know and will, at some point perhaps, need to be told. For some occasions, you can get by, but for continued interactions over weeks and months, you will have to contend with the idea that until they do, part of you is always putting on another element of the performance. You are meeting, in some way, what they expect to see. They do not know the real you and until they do the relationship is a stunted thing, unable to fully blossom. But will it be worth it? Do you have the energy to go through it again for the potential of what this relationship could be?

Ultimately, that is for you to decide for each new case.

I can pass for a cis woman. Even though doing so should not impact my validity as a transgender person, we live in a binary society for the moment and doing so helps me live under the radar until I deem otherwise. But that does mean that whenever I meet someone new or I get eyed up on the street I must ask whether they can see it or not. Do they know I am transgender? Is that why they are looking at me? Or are they objectifying me because of ingrained misogynistic permissions? How will they react if I tell them? Will they say they guessed or will they want to distance themselves from me? How will either make me feel? Am I scared that they can see through me, or will they hurt me for, in their eyes, being duped?

In the end, I have found it helpful to have three different approaches depending on the situation.

The first is for fleeting meetings. When I encounter someone in a passing fashion or maybe only a few times, such as a familiar delivery person or a builder whose round for a week or so doing work on the property, I will keep it to myself. They will be gone soon and it is not worth the effort or risk to let in a stranger onto something they could use as a point of attack.

The second is for acquaintances on the fringes of the social circle, such as your employer, hairdresser or beautician – those familiar enough that you will see them regularly over an extended period of time. For them, unless it is vital to the arrangement, such as for my beautician who is doing my electrolysis work, I once again keep the news to myself. I do not know whether we will remain in touch or for how long. Life can easily go separate ways and the tides take them far away. And then, if things do go sour, I do not get hurt as it is not me at fault but instead their assumed image of me.

However, should the topic naturally come up in conversation, then I would tell them. For example, I came out to work when the news was being particularly transphobic and we were in need of allies, so I did a roll call with my heart on my sleeve to stir some awareness. There is less risk when it is someone familiar and the topic being on the wind acts as an icebreaker, showing that they are aware and willing to discuss it. Then, speaking from a point of lived experience, it allows me to educate where necessary and provide a perspective they might not otherwise have had. It also helps clear the air for what might be a longer-term arrangement, allowing for greater ease in the future.

And the third is for close friends and potential partners. Here, I am up front and open from the outset. I lay all my cards on the table so that anyone who wishes to get that close to me knows. This initially helps filter out those who would not be accepting of it and allows through the open-minded, but it also means that I can take part in that relationship as me, one-hundred percent from the beginning. There is no protective performance with one foot out the door, no feeling things out or hedging my bets, ready to cut and run without costing myself too much. I am there, all in from day one. It makes the connection stronger and trust more reliable.

This is how I came out and how, over time, I fashioned my life. But it is not all social and emotional. There are practical and administrative elements to consider.

On a more official note, for those who have a job and will need to reconcile that with their new gender, thankfully the law is on your side. Due to anti-discrimination acts, an employer is unable to use gender identity or sexual orientation, as well as race, religion or ethnic background as a reason for letting you go. As a result, most businesses now have the mindset of acceptance, if not always understanding, and will hold onto you by the work you can give.

For me, I waited until after my probationary period just in case I needed the law at my back. I really need not have waited. Despite the relative youth and small size of the company for whom I worked at the time; they accepted me. They made a real effort to get my details changed on their domain as quickly as possible. My boss even called me up to say it affected nothing.

As a sales writer, I was lucky that my job allowed me to work from home, but for those who work in an office and have to commute to work, this will be a struggle you will need to undertake and overcome. Public transport was trying for me, the interrogation of halogen spaces. It took a long time for it to become routine, but even now I can feel out of place or under the spotlight, especially during busy hours with boisterous crowds.

It may be worth asking for some change to your working circumstances to aid in this. If the COVID pandemic has taught us anything, it is that more people can work from home than initially assumed and can work well under such situations. Also, understanding of LGBT+ people is pervading ever further into the corporate world, with more and more taking an effort to represent and educate.

While it may seem daunting, I have found it to be an accepting place due to its inherent pragmatism. If they want you, they will do whatever they can to keep you. But you will have to contend with the old hats of sexism and misogyny which, despite all best efforts, still exist in one form or another.

Lastly, I will talk about professional help.

As I mentioned earlier, when I came out, my parents advised that I speak to someone. Perhaps it was in some attempt to have someone make me realise the error of my ways or ensure I was certain. Either way, I sought out the psychiatrist at my university's mental health service while I was still a student there.

For some, this may be something you will want to try, to gain a sounding board, to speak ideas through and get an outside perspective. If that is the case, I would recommend it. They know what they are talking about and, for the most part, only want to help, and from those trained on these issues such help can be invaluable.

But it has to be your choice. You need to know why you are going and what you hope to achieve. And choose the therapist that is the best for you. I have seen a few in my day and some were not trained on transgender issues and thus tried to link everything back to gender even when it was not relevant. They were hunting for problems and directing me where I believe they wanted me to go rather than where I needed. I did not trust them. They were not there for me, for my best interests, but instead just to fix another problem before getting paid. I therefore could not open up and gain the benefit I might have otherwise.

Sadly, as of the time of writing, conversion therapy is still a legal practice in the United Kingdom. We have a tendency to listen to experts regardless of their biases or outside interests. We can take their word over ours because surely they know what is best. They wear fancy coats and have a certificate on their wall.

While I was not exposed to explicit conversion therapy, some part of me does wonder why my parents made me go. Were they helping me or hoping to help themselves? Talk me through it or talk me out of it? Perhaps I would understand it was all just a phase and things could go back to the way they were.

Because there are always agendas at play, be they from the other side of the desk or from those encouraging you to be there. They may only be subconscious in nature but are no less insidious for it. Stay true to what you want to ask and what you want to know. Have a goal in mind and do not be swayed. Search for answers, not destinations. Use them as a way to figure things out and do not let them or anyone else dictate things for you. This is your journey. These are your feelings and no one knows them better than you.

For me, the person I saw while at university said something that stuck. This is something I have mentioned before and will no doubt mention again.

They spoke about the labels we let ourselves be given, especially when we are young and unsure of who we are. They said there is no sign stamped onto my forehead that defines who I am; it is by my choices and my actions that I am defined and even those can change over time. Any label is there only for the moment, to describe how you feel most comfortable and to accurately represent you as you are now. They are not there for the rest of your life. Through my pubertal years, while my body went through hell, I retreated into the safety of the identity I fashioned for myself to please others. But now I am in control, and I will not let myself be left behind again.

While it was hard letting go of the familiar safety net and all the relationships it supported, it was undeniably exciting to think of where I could go from here and to make the most of the time that I had now to live. But to get there, I had to say those words. I had to make it real.

And I am glad I did.

Chapter Three

Strangers, Friends and Family

What friends you have effects the kind of reaction you will get. For me, my friendship group's average age was around twenty-five when I came out, so they were naturally quite a liberal and progressive bunch and only wanted the best for each other. They were accepting and allowed me all the space I needed to experiment and find out who I was during this change. But it took a lot longer for me to reconnect with older friends, those who had known me longer. Part of me was worried it would be more difficult to reconcile the 'new' me with the image they had previously held. It could render false all the time we had spent together, as though they never really knew me. Would they even want me back?

As I have mentioned, I always felt like an outsider and maintained a stock image, one that could be relied upon, so as to not risk the little I did have. If I suddenly became a different person, how could I fit into that same role? Or would the script reassert itself and diminish the progress I was making? I did not want to take any step backwards, not after finally going forward and living for myself rather than for those around me.

But when I think about it, I still have all the same qualities. I am empathetic, conscientious, interested in science and music, a devout nerd and with the same dreams, fears and need for connection. Except now each of these has been notched up to eleven and with a true chance of taking part as the real me. Before, it was a shadow going through the motions. Now, I can actually see them through. I am finally alive and ready to live.

I am still me – there is just more of me.

Though all this does come with the caveat that I have never liked people knowing my weaknesses. It is not that I am ashamed of them, but that I do not want to burden them with my faults. Then, the snake in my mind tells me that when I am alone it is because I am not good enough. I am not worthy.

We all have our demons. As hard as they can be to conquer, many stay with you far longer than they are welcome. Mine still do, from time to time. The unchanging rock you do not need to worry about. The one thing that will always be there for you. The one thing that will never disappoint you. Nothing else than what you need me to be.

I was fine on the outside.

But by being this person, I took from my friends the chance to know me properly just so I could maintain this perfect image, nor upset their world view or my minute boundaries of recognition. I found security, affirmation and faux company in this illusion. But because I did not need them for anything more than the presentation, they did not need me for anything more than the same.

Removed from that, I was alone. And that cost me. It cost me a decade.

I did not come out to put on them my insecurities or tribulations, or to force a 180-degree shift. I did so to offer forwards the 'me' I always should have been. I wanted to let them know who I was and, as a result, realise a more lasting friendship. For how could I give myself to experience were I nothing else but the actor, the bit part raising their head for a line or two? It would all pass me by in the rolling daily drama.

But expressing yourself means expressing the bad as well as the good, and when you express yourself, you are open to change. We could now support each other and grow stronger as a result. They are my guides and help me learn from myself, and I have the opportunity now to be the same for them. And together we will go places I never would have thought possible.

You may lose friends along the way, but for those you keep, it is a testament of trust to let them see beyond the fortress you built for them. Those are the friends worth keeping.

Yet, in every category of life, there is one element you will need to recognise, and that is the grief others may express after you come out. Whether you change drastically or not, there will still be a period of adjustment, a time when what they believed was true is now no longer, and this will manifest in the grief of loss.

It can be hard to bear having those you love crying over the person they want back, the person they cannot have back, even though you are right there with them. You may be there, finally complete and feeling more alive than ever, but they will mourn just the same. As much as it hurts, these emotions are real. My mother wept over her son while I sat there, wondering whether I had made a mistake, if I had hurt her or ruined myself in the process. By coming out as a transgender woman had I made myself inherently unlovable, even to my own mother?

She thought it was some mistake on her part that had pushed me so far away, causing me to no longer be the son she had raised for so much of her life. And it hurt her, even more, to know that I had been suffering in silence for most of mine. That is why she found it so difficult to accept. I tried every way I knew how to dissuade her from her guilt and grief. I tried describing the transition as an 'as well as' rather than an 'instead of', and that it was because of her love and motherhood that I had been allowed the opportunity to discover who I was, and now had the chance to express it.

My father, on the other hand, is a pragmatic man and rolled with the punches. But not every father will be the same. Yours may not wish to lose the other 'man of the family', or your mother may be happy to 'gain a daughter' and have another way with which to connect. And my brother gave me the 'it is just a phase speech' before relenting. It took many months, several speeches, and even some swearing to eventually get through to them, but we did make it in the end. And as a family, we are closer now than we have ever been.

Each dynamic will be different. There are as many stories and permutations, identities and struggles as there are transgender people to go through them. The key is to neither dismiss these feelings nor let them cut too deep. Each person will work through it in their own time and in their own way. You must remain strong and sure while they come to discover the new normal and find peace in that because you will need to be there when they are ready to move on and start living again. You cannot turn back and undo everything you have discovered for their sake. Such platitudes will only build a half-life for all involved. You will be left watching the world outside the window, wondering what could have been were you able to connect with it as a complete person instead of a manifestation of guarded expectations.

And this is what makes coming out to family such a different and difficult endeavour. Everything is amplified a hundredfold. The subversion. The grief. The courage. The loss. The doubt. The rediscovery. But hopefully, this has helped contextualise the thoughts family members can experience during such a process. Do not feel frustrated, as I know I did when they need time to figure it all out. While the transition is yours, it affects everyone in its own subtle way. Compassion and patience can go a long way to reaching a place of love and reunion.

Strangers, on the other hand, might not be so friendly or politically minded. While the transgender experience has gained a lot more coverage in recent years, not all of it has been truthful or kind, and for many, it is still quite a distant thing. Most people can go years, or perhaps their whole lives, not having met, seen, heard from or interacted with a transgender person. As a result, they can see it as something purely cosmetic or bizarre, a lifestyle choice meant for attention and nothing more. With this outlook, they can give themselves permission to ridicule it because they do not understand it. And the amount of flak you get can change from neighbourhood to neighbourhood and on how 'well you present', to put it haphazardly.

I will get into this more in later chapters on the art of dressing, walking, make-up and the use of the voice, but presenting as your desired gender is a key part of the transition. Unfortunately, we still live in a binary society and most of the world is dictated by assumptions based on these two extremes. To that end, by presenting well, you can avoid a lot of the pitfalls and daily interrogations because you fall within these assumptions and therefore do not rock the boat enough to draw attention. But this only reinforces that binary outlook.

When I first came out, I dressed and presented myself in a hyperfeminine manner, almost to try and distance myself from how I used to be and perhaps justify that I was a woman now. In its way, however, this was also something of a role put on for the benefit of others. In time, I found my own niche within the spectrum, an androgynous middle ground where I can be myself without excessive effort and without worrying about the opinions of my stranger-filled peerage.

I learned, in time, that presenting does not equal validity. A transgender person is no more or less transgender because they choose to present one way over another or if they have difficulty meeting the beheld standards of their desired gender and its social norms. Presentation is about uniting one's own internal identity with their external perception to finally silence the dysphoric voice in their mind and give themselves a chance to attempt life whole at last.

Within these binary endpoints to which so many of us are still bound, despite our best efforts and hard-fought epiphanies, I yet reside, seen and accepted as female. I do not mistake my fortune in that regard, because even though I understand all of the above, it does sometimes make life easier to hide within assumptions rather than face opposition to the definition with every step. Because of this, I have barely received any negativity out in the wider world.

This nearly always comes down to sexist heckling. Most walks involve a look or two, sometimes an overt catcall and on occasion a driver using their horn to make themselves known. I have been propositioned at bus stops, had cars stop to try and pick me up, and misogyny on clear display in the workplace. The issue comes when their sexism is not clear. I cannot tell whether they are looking at me because they are discriminating against me for being transgender or if they are objectifying me because I am a woman. Perhaps it is both. Perhaps it is neither. Either way, every journey outside is tinged with an element of worry, anxiety and a furtive look over my shoulder. Even now.

I was hoping to outgrow it and become strong enough to deal with it, but it follows me still, this deep-seated insecurity. It is not just that I fear that I will be targeted for being transgender, it is that having entered into the female world later than normal, I am more aware of institutionalised sexism. Having been a victim of it in the office and then my father waving it away as my fault made me cry at the injustice. How can this still be happening? And then there is that fear. Will I be beaten up? Will I be raped? Will I be killed? For being a woman? For being a transgender woman? Just one on its own can be enough.

So, I try and walk with my head held high and confidence in my step. I was raised with the belief that I was male and so inherited the security of patriarchal protection. In a way, it carries through to this day, in my stride, in my gaze, in my aim. The authority of being in charge was instilled into me by the society in which I lived without me even knowing it, and even though it is a failing of the society that it teaches such lopsided rules, I do find it amusing I now use its lessons to ward away those who would think to pry me with their looks.

Though that being said, I have had my gender questioned once. I was in the frozen aisle at Sainsbury's during the early days of my transition just going about my weekly shop. I accidentally bumped into someone while browsing and quickly apologised. Something must have given me away – perhaps my voice, as I had not perfected it at that time – but they asked if I was a man. And then the world went cold. I was numb, illuminated by a spotlight, laid bare and under assault, and all I could think was to stagger away in retreat. To hide once more and slowly stitch myself back together after so easily being pulled apart.

I do remember hearing their partner giving them an earful as I left, and they later came to say sorry while I was in the checkout queue. But the damage had been done. Years of work rendered moot in a moment, all my effort was undone and the person everyone still saw was the person I was trying to escape. For as much as I tightened my armour, polished my brass and rehearsed my tune, would anything truly matter more than what I had been assigned at birth? Could I ever be anything else? Was I doomed to have that rotting thing inside of me for the rest of my life? The 'real' me.

This terror extends to and infects every aspect of my life. I cannot help but compare myself to cis women, especially those hypersexualised versions portrayed in media, and find myself inadequate. There are many days where I am convinced that the most base approximation of being a woman is but a mere aspiration I will never attain. There is an inherent difference I will never be able to shake. Because beneath everything there is the 'original' me tainting everything I wish to be.

Whenever I am out in public, especially alone, the most accurate way I can describe the feeling is that I am the star of a poorly reviewed musical and the world is my audience. They snicker behind the binary lights, while I have to struggle on with my own doomed act. The worse I feel, the more piercing their stares and how ravenously their laughter gets under my skin.

Yet I know it will not last. Nothing ever lasts. And I only feel this way because I live in a binary society and am constantly pressured to meet its standards rather than being allowed to live on my own. When I can find the distance between me and the strangers out there and their billboard judges, I remember that I am the bizarre mixture of everything that makes me who I am. It makes me unique.

Each day, society progresses and it becomes easier to stand unaltered in its presence and feel a little less out of place. And I am a part of that, I will progress with it, and I will not let them bend me back to my old role! I will not give them the vulnerabilities they need to prove their jests, because transitioning is more than just skin-deep. It is a way of thinking that promotes far more than those fading preconceptions and relics of an outmoded philosophy under which its advocates will one day be buried.

There is the formation of a person beneath all this.

It is slow. It takes time. And I will find my own slice of the spectrum to call my own and find contentment in that. I am not there yet and from time to time the snake yet bites and its venom yet stings. But progress is always being made. Progress, not perfection, as I have often been told.

But everyone has a place here should they wish it. Here, in a mode of acceptance, community, diversity and expression, in whatever form they find most comfortable.

Straight. Cis. Transgender. Non-binary. Asexual. Pansexual. Religious. Atheistic. From every race and ethnic minority. Because I do not want to see happen to them what nearly happened to me. I do not want to see anyone else left behind.

We know our roles so well that they can be hard to leave. Trust me, I know what that can be like. But there is an infinity of places within the spectrum. There is room enough for all. For our friends. For our families. For every stranger, we pass on the street. And for us. We can be the hardest person to convince that we belong, and doubt may rally from time to time, but once attained I promise such lodging will be worth it.

And in that way, these pages are perhaps my fumbling attempt to pass on to whoever might need it the same assurance I have fought to find. It has taken time for me to reach this point. I trip and I stumble. I weaken, crumble, and break. And I know that I have got further to go. But there is room enough for me to reform a hundred times over and keep on growing. Unique and unbridled, to the best of my abilities. I have my spot on the spectrum, with a community by my side to greet me and keep me company. Hopefully, I will see you there too.

Chapter Four

Dressing

Writing about the transgender experience is inherently difficult. This is not because of the intimate subject matter, though that does present its own unique set of challenges, but because by definition it comes from a realm of pure abstraction. For as much as I have tried to distil it down to logic and reason, I am unable to determine why identifying as a different gender is as liberating as it is and why such freedom is anchored around the gender.

But while the deeper meaning may yet be lost to me, perhaps even unknowable, the steps to get there are a little more certain. I only wish that when I was first exploring my new gender I had had someone to guide me. Everything you are about to read, and have already read, I was forced to figure out for myself. I was alone in my trial. There was no resource or guidebook I could draw from, just nearly eight years of lived experience, as of the time of writing.

In that vein, we are finally stepping away from the psychological side to the physical, that of dressing and presenting. Here, I am going to examine mostly the logistics of how this works, the effort it takes and the results that can be achieved. I will dabble into the mental side, but I covered a lot of this in the previous chapter.

The true difficulty of presenting is that this is what most people will see. Unless they are acquainted with you or have known a transgender person in the past, they are not going to be privy to the mental battle I have done my best to already describe. They will only know it as something cosmetic, nothing more meaningful than fashion.

They do not see the struggle of living every day knowing something is wrong but not understanding what it is. They do not realise what it is like to wake up to the fact that the view you once held of yourself is, if not wrong, at least incomplete. They do not see our fear as we stand on the precipice, shamed into silence. They do not see our pain as we do nothing but go along with the script they scribe for us. They do not see our doubt as we look into the hurricane and wonder if there is anything on the other side. They do not see the nights spent staring at the ceiling trying to reconcile disparate identities. They do not see the courage it takes to step off into the storm. And they do not see the resolution we achieve.

Being transgender is not about becoming someone new, it is about aligning our outward presentation to that of our internal evolution. We go through the transition not because it is a phase, a fad or a piece of fashion. We transition because it is the state in which we have found our most potent means of communicating who we are. With it, we can maintain our agency and explore the full reaches of that potential and then pass it onto those we love. We transition because it is our entryway into life. We transition because otherwise, we might as well not be here.

And part of that journey is finding one's own presentation style, the mode in which the above is most comfortably and effectively expressed.

That being said, the idea of presenting, or 'passing', is not ideal. Our merit as transgender individuals should not be determined by our ability to appear cis, yet there are two caveats to this, as I touched upon in the previous chapter.

One is the social preoccupation with binary gender norms and how presenting can make the journey easier. Whether you feel sacrificing the integrity of the process itself is worth it I will leave it up to each of you. The other is that presenting is more about finding a sense of self-comfort, that merging of the internal and external. For some, that might be appearing as the stereotypical image of the gender as which they identify, while for others that could be discovering some completely new style and state of being. As with everything to do with the transition, it is up to the individual, with as many solutions as there are people trying to find them.

When I started, I was in the former camp, always feeling most comfortable presenting as your average cis female. This has shifted a little more into the androgynous valley between the two binary extremes, but I still adopt a mostly feminine persona day-to-day, especially when I dress up for social events and nights out.

But how do you present?

For this chapter, we will focus on the clothing aspect, dressing from the perspective of someone assigned male at birth, as that is what I know best.

I will start with getting the shape. But please be warned that we will be looking into some details here and discussing some of the more intimate subjects of the transition process. For that reason, I will put here a 'Not Safe for Work' label so you are aware of where we will be going. And I am going to include as many details as I can, mainly as a guide for anyone going through something similar and who might need a few pointers. It can be hard to know where to start, so it is my hope that having it laid out simply, clearly and without bias or implied taboo should make it easier for those who need it to start their own physical transition process.

On top of that, for those who are not transgender, I also want to destigmatise the subject so you are aware of the process, the language and the feelings involved. That way, you can more openly discuss it and provide support and assistance, or just understanding where necessary to those that need it.

This whole book, in a way, is my attempt to create a safe space where anything and everything related to the transgender experience can be broached and discussed. To that end, I really hope you find it useful. Because there is no need to feel shame or embarrassment regarding anything already discussed or on the cards for the coming pages. These are stages everyone must go through in their own way to uncover the fully realised person at the end of it. Do not let the usual notions of social acceptability dictate you or stop the progress you have made.

The first step to living reality is to address it with pride.

So, with that warning done, on with the practicalities of dressing.

Tucking is the simplest place to start. It is a technique that will last for at least a few years. If you wish to tuck, you will be doing so either until you undergo gender confirmation surgery or indefinitely otherwise. I am going to go into detail to describe how you do it here, though you can also watch tutorials on YouTube or find other online resources that outline it as well. But as a note, they often mention something called a 'gaff' to hold everything in place afterwards, but I have found a tight pair of knickers with a wide gusset works just fine and is less obtrusive.

So, how to tuck? First, you will want to pinch the head of the penis and pull it back gently between your legs, positioning it in between your testicles so they bulge out a little. Then, holding the penis in place, gently press up with your fingers on the base of the testicles, slotting them into the pelvis from where they originally dropped during puberty.

This will feel weird at first, like a jolt of not quite pain. Your body will question what you are doing, but after a few times, everything will calm down as your body gets used to it. After a few weeks, and certainly months of doing it every day, it will become quick and easy, just part of the routine. Then, you will need to press your legs together to hold the tuck in place while you pull on your knickers, and there you go.

Though I do need to include a medical disclaimer here. By tucking over long periods, especially over the course of years and living a generally active life, you will be subjecting sperm to a prolonged increase in temperature, which can cause infertility or a general lack of fertility. If you go through the transition process, you will be required to consider gamete storage before starting hormone treatment, so you may wish to do this earlier if you are worried about having a surrogate child in the future. It may be good to get them on ice before there is any risk put their way. When I froze mine, after four years of tucking, they did detect a decrease in number, but not enough to cause problems.

The second part of getting the body shape is the breasts. Before hormones help grow natural breasts, forms are easy to acquire. When I used them, I found mine on Amazon, but there are plenty on eBay also. Search for 'cross-dresser breast-forms' and you should find some from a range of brands in different sizes and price brackets. I used the brand *Forever Young*. They were well-priced and of good quality, usually between £20-£50 depending on the size. If properly tended to, a pair can easily last a year or more.

I will say that it may be prudent to not get too excited and go for an overlarge pair. My advice would be to choose one that suits your body shape. The average breast size for a cis female is around a C-cup, depending on chest-size. If in doubt, this is probably your best bet to start with. Thanks to several years at the gym during my teens, I began the transition with a large chest size, especially around the latissimus dorsi muscles, meaning it totalled about thirty-eight inches when the average is thirty-four inches. For this reason, I got myself D-cup-sized forms and they fit perfectly.

Also, forms allow you to almost preview what breast-size will work for you if you decide to get breast augmentation surgery further down the line.

The most accommodating piece of clothing to support them is an underwire bra. The forms can then slot into the cups and be held in place without further need for tape or wraps, though these are also an option should you need them.

However, the downside of always needing a bra is that it can get uncomfortable to wear over long days – though you will not be alone in experiencing that. It can also preclude certain shoulderless or backless items of clothing. When shopping, you will need to do so with bra-straps in mind.

That, in short, is how you get the shape.

Wigs are something else you may wish to consider, but this is trickier to do so online. You can find wig-stores out there in most town centres, but unless you have the budget, resources and talent of a Hollywood costume department, they are never going to look the same as natural hair. If you have a naturally feminine face, you are probably better styling your hair into a pixie cut of some kind and taking the time to grow it out. This way, it will all blend together more effectively and help present a single, unified and natural image.

As time has gone on, I have been getting my hair cut shorter and shorter and leaving it as it is. In a way, I have almost the same hair I did before the transition because it seems to work for me better than any wig. I would recommend exploring both options and seeing which produces the best result for you. There are also transgender-friendly stylists out there that may be able to guide you in a more specific direction, based on your facial structure, hair colour and composition, and desired outcome.

In the early days of the transition, I chose a long, auburn wig. I used this to frame my face and hide my shoulders, which at the time were larger than desired. I only used it when I presented for social occasions, such as a night out, back when I had not yet reached the stage of presenting all day every day. When I did, I ditched the wig for several reasons.

Firstly, in daylight, it did not hold up the same as under a nightclub's lighting. Second, it was itchy and uncomfortable to wear for long periods. Thirdly, it left my hair in quite a state by the end of it. And lastly, I did not want to rely upon a wig to be able to present. I wanted to be, as best I could, just me. And this was part of achieving that. It served me for a while, but I then moved on as my transition took me in different directions. As it was always meant to be, it was a journey, with no fixed end point, but a continual evolution towards what most accurately and comfortably represented me at that moment.

But I will talk more about hair in a future chapter.

For now, let us turn our attention to clothing.

Before I start, I want to give mention to dressing services. When I was starting to dress, I discovered there are those out there who help transgender people find their style. They even have make-up lessons. Search 'trans dressing service' in Google, perhaps with your location too, and see what is there. But if you want to go alone, I have picked up a few tips over the years. My main piece of advice would be to work with what you have got.

I am not a supermodel, and most likely never will be. Thanks to those years at the gym, I started the process with non-existent hips, quite broad shoulders, large back muscles and annoyingly defined biceps. Hormones did rectify this in time, but that was several years in the future. So, when I started dressing, I went with those areas of my body that I liked. I have got nice legs, a narrow waist, shapely clavicles and a slender neck. Therefore, I used these to pick my wardrobe for me.

Anything that cinches at the waist, such as high-waisted jeans or shorts, belted skirts or skater dresses, can be a good place to begin. By pulling in the waist they accentuate the hips and add to that curve, which is also highlighted when walking. High-necked shirts and turtlenecks are also good. They hid my shoulders while they were still overly muscular and disguised any evidence of the breast-forms I used. These also work well with short haircuts so can help fill in those early days before your hair grows out.

I also got my legs out a lot during the early days, so I used shorter-than-average shorts and skirts. This is perhaps part of that effort to prove myself a female by playing up to expectations a little, but I also just enjoyed the feeling and sensation. I like my legs. Having them out makes me feel more feminine. Yet, I also used them to detract attention from my face, which I was always paranoid would not hold up to scrutiny.

Casual dresses I found too baggy for my liking. I have a naturally thin frame, so these looked more like curtains to me draped from my shoulders. Instead, I turned to clothes that contained a decent proportion of viscose or elastane in them. You can find this when online shopping in the details section on store pages where they outline the material composition. Viscose and elastane mean that the item will conform to the body and this helped me achieve that feminine look more easily.

However, as mentioned earlier, anything with a low-cut neckline or that is backless is difficult because of the necessity of wearing a bra to hold in the forms. Shoulderless also falls into this category, but you might strike lucky and find something with enough support to hold up your bra without the need for straps.

As for what colour to go for, this will partly be directed by your natural style and taste, but I found a monochromatic scheme worked best for me as almost everything goes with white or black. Yet, whatever you choose, you will want to avoid double patterning, such as with a chequered shirt and a flower-print skirt as these can conflict and become garish.

Heels can be your friend, shaping your legs and getting your posture to accentuate the shape achieved through forms and tucking, but at the extremes, they can also make you look overly tall and off balance. I am 5'9", which is tall for a woman but not overly so, thankfully, but it does mean that if I go overboard with heels, as I am sometimes wont to do, I can be too tall for my own liking. I tower over those around me and cause myself to stand out too much. Smaller block-heel shoes are a good middle ground here and there are plenty of options out there. Though, if your shoe size is larger than eight, you will need to search specialised stores, as this is above the limit of most common chains' stock.

The last thing to note is that, as much as it angers me, lingerie is a complete no-go. Anything frilly does not have the support necessary to hold a tuck. But, once hormones have caused natural breasts to grow, a lace camisole or bralette can be a good alternative to the classic lace bra. Knickers and thongs, however, will always remain an issue without the confirmation surgery. You need something with a wide gusset to act almost like a taut hammock to hold in the tuck.

Very little about transitioning is simple.

My last warning would be to not be convinced by models in magazines or on clothing websites.

Unfortunately, until hormones and surgery are out of the way, even for cis women, models present an almost unattainable aspiration and expectation of what a woman can and should look like.

This is part of the challenge of living in the hypersexualised world we do where everything feminine is about emphasising the most sexual characteristics to a practically unfeasible degree. I know I feel diminished when I compare myself to their doctored and airbrushed presence, but it heartens me to know that I am far from alone in that folly. Nearly every woman, cis or otherwise, experiences some fear of inadequacy when looking at storefront models, billboards, and Hollywood girlfriends.

But as hard as it can be, all I can say for this is to do your best to put it out of your mind and accept that what looks so good on them may not work for you. It is about dressing smart, using everything I have outlined above as guidance to what might become your new look.

Though I will not lie, it is endless fun discovering your style. And when you have found it, flaunt it.

Flaunt you.

Chapter Five

Hair, Hair Removal and Make-Up

Similar to the previous chapter, this one will focus more on the logistical and practical side of the transition and presenting. I hope that it can serve as a guide, using my experiences and what I have learned over the years to help those who are just starting out and do not know how to begin their journey. We all need a few pointers. I only wish that I had been in a position to receive any when I was at this stage, either from a big sister I do not have or a more accepting mother that was not available at the time. Either way, I have found myself in a place where I am happy with my appearance, and hopefully, I can help achieve the same for you.

Though, I must say all this will be from the perspective of a transgender woman because that is what I am and that is what I know. There will be other resources out there that cover other avenues of the transition. I highly recommend that wherever you lie on the spectrum and whatever your desired endpoint, it can only help to become well read on the subject and understand all its nuances and possibilities. There is always more to learn and consider, to help your own transition, those you love and the needs of the wider community.

My aim is that this book will cover every step of the transition process, the psychological as well as the physical. While it will use my own journey as a basis, I sincerely hope that readers of all flavours and situations can draw something from its pages to aid them. It was something I know I could have used myself when I was first starting to explore and dress.

We will start in earnest, picking back up the conversation on hair that I touched upon in the previous chapter. I covered wigs slightly, so I will focus on hair this time.

What hair you decide to go with is really up to you. I started by growing my hair out, but I could never get myself beyond the awkward phase. It never quite fit me. Over time, I eventually circled back round to having short hair. But I later learned from my stylist that to grow out your hair you need to have it cut and trimmed regularly to shape its growth. With that in mind, if you wish to have long hair, it may be worth getting yourself booked into a local salon to talk it through with the people there, as they will know how best to work with your hair and vision.

I do know that this can be a massive obstacle and a place of intense fear and worry. I remember being terrified about going to a salon for the first time, and nervous for every subsequent trip during those early days. Not only was it a new group of people, meaning I had to contend with the coming-out questions I outlined earlier, but I knew I would feel inadequate presenting before the stereotypically stylised staff. And if I went presenting as male, I would feel out of place, like an intruder, and that I had not progressed as much as I had wished. My life was still a dichotomy, preserved in limbo.

I was reminded somewhat after the fact that there are hairdressers that can come to your home and work with you there. It also gives you a chance to correspond with them beforehand and let them know the situation so you can break the ice and both work towards the same outcome. This might be something you wish to explore.

In the intervening years, I have since managed to go to salons and found them welcoming and helpful. I also came out as transgender to my stylist recently. The conversation allowed for it quite naturally and they were rather nonplussed. As with many organisations these days, brand identity and being on the right side of society is crucial to attracting and keeping custom. Unless they are unconscionably bigoted, which is thoroughly unlikely, they will accept you and do their best to help because it suits their needs as well as yours.

The last word I will say on hair is to reiterate a point I made earlier, and that is to work with what you have. Keep things as simple and as natural as possible for day-to-day life. By all means, go extravagant should the situation call for it, but for everyday living, find what style works best for you. For me, that happened to be a short, almost boyish cut that then grows out into a kind of pixie cut. Creating a single, unified image and style is key to finding the best way to outwardly present your internal identity and help guard yourself against the million unspoken jibes of our modern world.

Moving onto hair removal, there is a lot to cover in this subject as it can include different methods for all areas of the body. I will begin with the legs, as these are the simplest to do using your own initiative.

There are many beauty parlours and salons that can offer this service, and there are also home remedies if the idea of the salon, like before, is too much for you at that time. But also similar, I have found all parlours to be accepting and eager to help, accommodating of its unique set of challenges. Many have even encountered transgender people before and are well versed fonts of wisdom.

Now, the amount of hair a person has and how it grows can change drastically due to many factors, such as age, health, diet and genetics. I started off with quite hairy legs but very little elsewhere, such as on my back, chest and arms. Therefore, my first step was to shave my legs completely using a hair removal cream, such as Veet or Nair. It worked remarkably well and broke the back of what needed to be done. That first assault is the most labour-intensive and such creams are a good initial way of, in your own time, painlessly, if not odourlessly, ridding yourself of long, coarse hair.

After this, it becomes a battle of maintenance.

For this protracted campaign, there are two main methods to use. You can either stick to the razor and spend a half-hour in the shower each week or two, or you can wax with at-home kits or at beauty parlours. I went with parlours and thankfully had a very understanding beautician in whom I could confide my reasons for being there.

Even though waxing does hurt, it has many benefits. The hair remains gone for longer, about four-six weeks, and when it comes back, it does so finer and softer. So even if you decide to only do a six-session course, it will help in the long run and make shaving easier down the road. If done for longer, it can rid large areas of hair permanently, but this takes years, sometimes decades to achieve. Hormones will also help in this regard, but I will leave that for a future chapter.

The only caveat to mention with waxing is that many full-leg waxes also include work on the bikini line and not every parlour is trained to accommodate the assigned-male-at-birth anatomy. Due to this, you can either forgo the bikini line with an explanation or not, as I have done in the past, or if you wish to have it waxed you can find a parlour that has the training to do so. This will usually require you to come out and explain your situation, but as I have noted throughout, they are bound to be accepting.

This then brings us to removing hair on the face, which comes with its own set of complications. Along with getting your legs waxed, I would recommend doing your eyebrows at the same time, to shape them. It can have a surprisingly noticeable effect on feminising the face, though I would emphasise not to go overboard and have too much removed or to chase social trends. After too much waxing or plucking, eyebrow hair does not return and if you go too thin you can be stuck with it.

I have spoken to many cis women who regret this aspect of their teenage beauty regime. I have thick, dark eyebrows that work for my face but can get untidy. So I have them shaped and arched, but not thinned that much. It keeps my look consistent and natural while gaining the benefits of the subtle, feminising treatment.

But to the crux of the matter, and that is facial hair. Before I began the transition, I was cursed with the ability to grow a fine beard, so when I chose to present, I had to wet shave and pray I did not cut myself. I sought permanent hair removal during the time I had between seeking a referral and my first appointment at the gender clinic. While some hair removal is available as part of the transition process through the NHS – with the focus being on the UK's system as that is what I went through myself – these have long wait times and are often at clinics far from home, with appointments set to suit them rather than you. It can therefore be more convenient to spend a little money, if possible, and find a private clinic close by that can fit you into your desired routine.

There are three methods of permanently removing facial hair: electrolysis, epilation or laser treatment. They each have their pros and cons and I will cover them individually below, but there are two points to note before I do.

The first is that every method will require you to grow out the hair for about a week beforehand. This can be disruptive to your ability to present, and it was for me, forcing me to present as a male for more time than I would like. This is something to be aware of when considering such treatments, but now that the COVID pandemic has made wearing masks expected and encouraged, this can be a solution.

The second is aftercare. Regardless of the method, there will be some damage to the skin based simply on what is being done. The amount will change, but I would encourage you to at least get into the habit of moisturising daily even when not near a session. This helps keep the skin healthy over time. It may also be worth investing in a full skin care routine, with cleansers, creams, moisturisers and anti-inflammatories. These latter ones are especially important to help heal the skin directly after treatment, with aloe vera creams and witch hazel gels recommended by professionals and available at pharmacies. I have found them effective in calming everything down afterwards.

Laser Hair Removal

This was the first option I chose. Most private clinics offer some form of laser hair removal and it has become increasingly popular in recent years. I went with the Harley Medical Group as there was one near me and I was happy with the results. It is a non-intrusive method that uses lasers to zap the bulbs of each hair. It can be used to quickly target wide patches of hair as the laser can be programmed to flash with different speeds and intensities. It does leave red blotches or scabs, but these heal over in a couple of days.

The only limitation of lasers is that it requires a colour contrast between the hair and the skin. This can mean that if you have dark hair and darker skin, or fair hair and fairer skin, there are some hairs that you simply will not be able to reach. For that reason, I found lasers to be a primary method for dealing with the broad areas of hair, such as on the cheeks, jowls and jawline, but ineffective against those around the lips and chin once the worst offenders are gone.

Another drawback of laser hair removal is that it is painful, especially on sensitive skin around the mouth. Some of those to whom I have spoken found it too painful for them to continue. The clinic will normally offer a free consultation, however, so you can try it out and see if it is for you. They will also test here if the lasers can target the hairs based on the contrast mentioned earlier.

Sessions usually occur a month apart, becoming more spread out as the course goes on and hair fades. The consultants, I have found, get people seeking hair removal for the transition quite often and were understanding when I told them why I was there. I had treatments for about two years but stopped when they reached all that they could achieve. I still have some hairs around the chin and lips and shave these areas most days. In the meantime, I searched for other options to deal with this obstinate lot.

Epilation

Epilation can only be found at beauty parlours and uses sonic vibrations to wiggle the hair bulbs free from the pores, which are then plucked using tweezers. Unlike electrolysis, the growth stage of the hair is more important here regarding whether the bulb will become freed or not, and it does not require the colour contrast of lasers.

However, after around eight months of treatment, with sessions spaced a month apart, I found no noticeable difference in the overall reduction. While the hair would stay away initially for about a week, it would return afterwards just as before, and over time there was no major change. This is also by far the most painful of the methods and almost unbearable on the upper lip and around the nose. I came out crying from nearly every session.

For these reasons, I would recommend against pursuing epilation as a method for permanent hair removal.

Electrolysis

This is the only method of hair removal that is covered by and available under the NHS, though only a set number of sessions are offered and these are not guaranteed to remove everything over the course. These sessions occur later in the transition process and only if you go through their system, which currently takes years to even attain an initial appointment. It is also more difficult to find in clinics outside the NHS as few commercial beauticians are trained in electrolysis.

Electrolysis involves heated needles that fry and cauterise the bulb of each individual hair, which is then pulled out using tweezers. It is a more targeted method and can take longer overall, but there are no hairs on which it is not effective. Though it has better long-term results, it can cause scarring due to its intrusive nature.

Having been through it myself, there is normally a five-seven day growth period prior and then three-seven days of recovery afterwards to allow the skin to cool down and heal. This does induce dysphoria having to deal with growing out the hairs and then dealing with the aftermath in an almost constant cycle, so whether this and the pain of the sessions themselves are worth the trade-off is up to the individual.

Currently, I have had over a year of electrolysis, with sessions spaced a fortnight apart, and have found the results mixed. It helped get rid of the straggling hairs left on the cheeks and jawline from the other methods, but the stubborn lot around the lips and chin are clinging on fervently.

Regarding pain, electrolysis is only moderately painful: a pinprick on the skin accompanied by a hot sensation for a few seconds afterwards, with the more sensitive skin on the upper lip reacting more. To me, it was the least painful method, outside of the dysphoria mentioned above. This is present in every method but has been more noticeable in electrolysis.

Of these three, I would therefore recommend using lasers as an initial way to rid yourself of the bulk, and then switch to electrolysis to focus on those stubborn areas or those hairs lasers cannot reach. You will need to consider your budget and where these options are available in your area, though this can be helped by using the British Institute and Association of Electrolysis (BIAE) website, which lists trained specialists and their locations. As with everything in the transition, it is neither simple nor cheap.

Over time, a course of laser treatments is several hundred to a thousand pounds, depending on the clinic and course, and individual electrolysis sessions cost about £20 each. And while I am on the subject, depending on what kind of medical coverage you can get and what surgeries you decide to have, the full cost of the transition can range anywhere from £3,000 to £30,000.

But do not feel daunted. This is spread out over the whole course and the bulk comes from optional surgeries that are not covered by the NHS. I will talk about these in a dedicated chapter for those who wish to know more about the various surgeries, but until now, the main costs include hair removal, buying clothes, and investing in styles and salon treatments.

These, however, are mostly recurring costs and are something you will need to incorporate into your monthly budget. In our world, being a woman is generally more intensive and costly, so be prepared for an increase in living costs once the transition is underway. This is an unstated benefit of coming out to and reconciling with family, as the financial and logistical support they can offer, such as for travel distances to various salons, clinics, and hospital appointments, can be instrumental at times.

But for now, we move onto make-up.

This is another factor that can change from person to person, depending on skin tone, face-structure and situation. While I no longer use make-up that much day-to-day, reserving it for more special occasions, it was a large part of my daily routine in the early stages of the transition and almost a necessity for me to feel confident presenting. I found that keeping it simple was better for everyday living and there are plenty of make-up tutorials on YouTube, many of which are transgender-specific. These would be a good source of knowledge that can be geared directly to your needs. That being said, I will cover the basics here based on what worked best for me and the eventual routine on which I settled.

Foundation

When I used foundation, I did so in two tones, one that matched my skin colour and another slightly darker. I used these together to subtly contour around my eyes to accentuate them more, as they are one of my better features.

The lighter tone I applied in a T-shape above the eyebrows and down the slope of the nose, then more wrapping under the eyes and around the mouth. The darker shade I placed at the top of the forehead and beneath the cheekbones, then blended the two into a smooth covering that I left to dry. When blending, be sure to match the foundation to the skin down the neck and behind the ears, especially if you have short hair, so as not to leave an obvious line between one and the other. There are contour face-maps online if you want a more visual guide.

Eyeliner

There are multiple types and colours of eyeliner based on your preference and dexterity. I use a black liquid eyeliner that is applied to the upper lash line. Eyeliner is tricky to use at first and takes a lot of practice, especially if you wish to go further and create wings that spread from the upper corners. It is also worth becoming proficient in using it with each hand for the corresponding eye, as relying on your dominant hand alone can make the process more difficult and cause the shaft of the brush to touch the nose, which can leave marks.

Over time, I became accustomed to the motion of the brush and found the shape and colour brought out my eyes in a way I liked. I use my pinkie finger as an anchor on my cheekbone and rotated my wrist around to help create the necessary arc. I sometimes combine this with pencil liner on the upper and lower waterlines to add a subtle thickening, but this needs to be reapplied several times throughout the evening as it gets rubbed off.

Mascara

Much to the chagrin of many female friends and partners over the years, I was blessed with startlingly long eyelashes. For that reason, mascara for me is quite easy to apply, but the secret is to build it up in layers while focusing on flicking the outer corner and curling it towards the far tip of your eyebrow. If you can get your eyeliner to match this from beneath, you can get a subtle effect that mimics a wing without the same level of hassle, opening the eyes to a striking degree.

Powder

Now that I no longer use foundation, I have turned to powder to produce the base coat for my skin, but it can also be used to even out the appearance on top of a layer of foundation. For both, I use the same routine. I repeat what I did with foundation but with two-tone powder instead. I focus mainly under the eyes and on top of the cheekbones with the light powder and then beneath the cheekbones with the darker powder to help emphasise that contouring effect. The care here is in not using too much and blending it in with the bare skin of your neck and behind your ears, and only subtly tracing out under the cheekbones with the darker powder, otherwise, it can look odd having two great shadows on your face.

Lipstick

Unfortunately, where my eyelashes succeed my lips do not. They are quite thin and not shaped that much, so I find them hard to work with, even after years of trying. For that reason, I stay away from lipstick most of the time. When I do use it, I use a light colour as a base, then layer up a darker one on top, though I find the change in shade between it and my skin too stark. It looks a little weird, for my features at least.

It is hard to describe how to use make-up outside of a visual medium, so YouTube and other online tutorials are vital in this regard. I know I relied upon them at the start. But hopefully, I have given you some ideas.

However, it does take some getting used to, having all this product on your face, how it changes your appearance, and how you come to view and interact with your face in close detail. It can also, at times, feel like an extension of the deception, a crutch to be relied upon, a mask you need to wear to feel accepted in the wider world.

To me, though, it was a realisation of form that hormones would eventually enable. It was a head start. As with dressing, it was one more piece to the puzzle that gave me the ability to take control of my life, one layer at a time.

Chapter Six

The Voice and the Walk

Over these last few chapters, we have examined how dressing, presenting and make-up can aid you in becoming comfortable in your own skin. These are the first elements to use when initially defining and refining your identity. They can change over time, and fluctuate in their style and impact, but they are tools to be used so that you can inhabit your life with power and agency. Yet there are two final pieces that help complete the ensemble when it comes to interacting with the outside world. This is through movement and speech, and I will begin with speech as it is the most personal and, because of that, the trickiest for fear of failure and embarrassment.

The best way to achieve a feminine-sounding voice is to gain advice from a professional vocal coach. These can be acquired privately, but as with hair removal, this may be too expensive or hard to locate within your area. In the UK at least, the NHS gender transition programme does include both individual and group vocal coaching sessions. These are available to sign onto once you have reached the gender identity clinic, though they do come with the usual caveats of waiting times, availability, long periods of travel and appointments assigned at perhaps inconvenient times, which you must make or risk losing your spot.

Having taken part in some of these sessions, I can attest that they can be a first port of call, but I do not believe they can cover the end-to-end change required. They help break the back of changing your vocal style and provide tips and pointers, establish confidence and routine, but a lot of the work must be done individually and through targeted training, so you can find what works best for you in terms of method and results.

The NHS' individual sessions establish your personal sound, and group courses work on phone calls and public speaking. There are also, as with most things, tutorial videos on YouTube with good advice.

Thankfully, having been in the theatre my entire life, with some rudimentary if mostly ineffective coaching in singing, I have always had control over my voice. Due to this, I made good progress adapting my voice to my new gender identity through my own techniques, familiarity with experimentation, and having long become used to it sounding strange to my ears. That being said, I did and still do encounter vocal dysphoria when I hear my voice recorded and played back, though I suppose that is common to everyone, transition or not.

And while there are stereotypical ideas of what a gendered voice may sound like, it is worth bearing in mind that the range of pitches can change drastically from person to person. A cis male may have a naturally high, soft voice, whereas a cis female may have something lower and more resonant. The voice alone is not a definition of gender but part of a person's individual identity, and it does not do well, as with many aspects of the transition, to strive for conformity if it risks your vocal or mental health. This should not be another element of performance to reach a socially defined ideal. The voice should be an extension of you, as natural as breathing.

The main method I used to adjust my voice was through a kind of vocal visualisation I developed to create different character voices during my acting days. I did this by imagining and then changing the point of origin for the sound when I spoke.

Before I began, I was quite a noticeable bass, so when I spoke the resonance would come from my chest, just behind the sternum. So, to find your spot, speak a random sentence and feel for where the sound is coming from in your body, where those vibrations originate, and imagine that as a point of light. You can then move this point by adjusting the muscles in your throat. Your facial muscles may also get involved, as can your posture. All this links together to get the pitch and timbre.

Instead of shooting off into a head voice, I shifted that point so it was pitching my voice at the roof of the throat, the sound then emerging from the back of the mouth rather than deep in my chest, the cavity there being what adds a lot of those resonant bass frequencies. This is a noticeably higher pitch than before but not so high as to sound forced. My voice has adapted over the years to this new level and

I can maintain a tenor range without much effort or thought.

The only warning I have is that most online tutorials I looked at when I was first starting out instructed me to use falsetto to train my voice to rest at a consistently higher pitch. This is something I have never found useful and it can actually make it harder to achieve what you want; it strains your voice and the forced nature does not sound convincing. To me, at least. Instead, this is attained through frequent and practical use more than anything else.

Another method I developed was to tense the muscles in the throat to lift the voice box as if in preparation to speak, but without actually talking. I established this to use on bus rides or while walking so the time was not wasted. It also helped maintain the progress created through sessions and in situ use, because, at the end of the day, the voice is governed by muscles and it is about training those muscles as you would for any other skill, be it exercise or learning an instrument. Over time, they will settle to the new level and stay there without having to force themselves or think about it too much.

Doing this has also meant the tone, timbre and intonation pattern of my voice has changed to match. Typically, women speak in softer tones with a more lilting pattern to their speech, whereas men are quite direct and perfunctory. This has not been a conscious choice I have made but rather it came naturally with the pitch and the change of the voice's source.

When it comes to creating your own voice, my advice would be not to try and emulate someone, such as a celebrity or a friend. Instead, it is best to discover the natural place where your voice likes to rest and leave it there. This will be the most comfortable and convincing, and the easiest to maintain over long periods of time without the voice becoming strained or tired.

It takes effort and a force of will to keep the voice consistent before it has had time to settle into its new place, and it can be frustratingly easy to slip back into what was for so long the familiar state. I hated the dissonance of falling into my old voice, just as I hated any step backwards. It reminded me that I still had a way to go, and that my life could yet be influenced by that old part of me. One that was no longer relevant or representative, yet for its origins and persistence seemingly the truer.

While I now no longer need to think about my voice when I speak, it was not always so. It used to be a battle for every word and sentence. I would sometimes hum under my breath to set my pitch before speaking, or do so afterwards in preparation for the next exchange. But nothing is infallible. In moments of laziness or surprise, it often returned to what was, at the time, its default state.

As mentioned, it was my voice that let me down the one time I had my gender questioned.

I remember the feeling well.

I could barely walk, my mind whirled, and everything went quiet but for my heart bursting out of my ears. The lights of the world were on me, stripping me bare and revealing all my games for the act I feared they were. Of course, I know this is not true. I am doing this to gain a form in which I can most freely give myself to life and receive life in return, but when someone can so accurately plunge a knife into a gap in your armour, it is hard to not believe that this is all for nought. That you are guarding something fragile. That you are still dependent upon an illusion that must remain intact. And that you can never escape the 'real' you. It will always be there for someone to see and use to define you.

Ultimately, finding your voice is part of finding the real you, but there will be no change overnight. It will take months of training and experimentation to obtain a voice that can be used in everyday conversation. And while it can be frightening to start for fear of taking that imperfect first step, it must be done for the destination to be reached.

For me, it took about three years to reach a subconscious level, and even then I found myself slipping occasionally when I was relaxed among my friends, a place where I did not feel the need to present so drastically. I do not know if I will ever overcome my vocal dysphoria when hearing it played back, but to my own ears at least, I am happy. I know I am accepted when I speak to strangers, shopkeepers, delivery people or even over the phone, without any other clues or indicators of my gender. But however you decide to approach this part of the transition, I wish you the best of luck. The end result can be quite surprising.

But following on from the voice, we go now onto the movement, both on the large scale and the small. Some may come as a natural extension of the voice, and may even serve to help direct the voice, but others will need the same level of a conscious effort to find, define and refine, at least at first.

Facial expressions do differ slightly between the typically associated binary genders. From my experience, women have more expressive features, especially around the eyes and eyebrows. To help with this, I first made a note to use the muscles around my eyes and ears to give my face a brighter, more open feel and an increased dynamic range to any expression I made. This has since worked its way into my standard repertoire.

You may have also heard the phrase: 'talk with your hands'. This is true, to some extent. In the broadest possible terms, where men like to make direct motions to reinforce their points, women have more sweeping gestures that almost dramatise whatever they are saying.

Such expansive gesticulations can also help guide the passage of your vocal inflections and add one more layer to creating the self-image you are trying to achieve.

To create these gestures, I find it useful to keep my elbows closer into my waist or chest, with my wrists slightly limp so my hands and fingers gain a greater fluidity. Of course, there are situations, such as business handshakes, where a limp wrist is not ideal, but this should help in more day-to-day scenarios.

Standing and posture is also a small aspect that should be considered. When I stand, I usually have my feet close together, heels almost touching with one pointed away from the other with my weight leant upon one leg. I sometimes stand with one foot forward while leaning upon the other in the rear, cocking the hip out somewhat to create a pose with more presence.

Leading directly on from this is the walk. The walk is one of the more important aspects of presenting as it will be what carries you through the daily social gauntlet. When it comes to cis members of a gender, there is a definite way of walking, defined by skeletal and anatomical differences. There are, of course, unique variations from person to person, so I am speaking here in terms of the stereotypical image.

Men tend to lead with the head and move with the shoulders, each one rocking back and forth, maybe even turning in circles depending on an individual's propensity to swagger. Their knees are normally slightly bent and apart and their feet point outward as they walk. It is quite a rigid movement, all told. Women are mostly the complete opposite. They lead with the chest, with the shoulders arched back and arms relaxed against their side instead of flowing with the saunter. And rather than their shoulders being the centre of rotation, it is their hips that move the most due to a naturally wider pelvis. Also, their legs are kept together more at the knees and their feet are pointed forward.

When walking, the temptation might be to overcompensate with the hips to create that desired sway, but this can be a little over the top depending on how much is put into it. But I found a secret while experimenting in my room. I did spend a few nights pacing trying to get it right, only managing about three steps at a time because I did not have that much space. And that secret was to completely ignore the hips and instead focus on the shoulders. But rather than moving the shoulders, I kept them utterly still. If you hold your shoulders still while you walk, your hips will work to naturally swing wider from side to side to keep your balance as you rotate from foot to foot. Couple that with a narrower stance and a gliding motion, and it all seems to fall into place.

Now, an understated point when it comes to walking is footwear. What shoes you have can make a big different to how you travel, depending on their shape, padding, incline and other such factors. Due to this, I would like to mention the typical shoes that I have found most useful.

Most days, I wear flats or pumps. Sometimes, if I am in an adventurous mood, I would swap these out for some block-heeled ankle boots. The former provides little impact, but the latter, due to the slight heel, helps with the sway of the hips I established earlier. Then, for more social occasions, I usually split myself between block-heeled sandals or the classic stiletto look. The former offers the same advantages as the boots while being easier to walk in, while the latter presents a more stereotypically feminine image but does have some negatives.

The first of these is due to height. If you are like me and are transitioning from assigned-male-at-birth to a female gender identity, then you will most likely be taller than the average woman. If you add heels onto this, you can reach the point where you are over and above six-foot, and this can draw unwanted attention to you, perhaps working against the presentation you may be trying to achieve. At 5'9" myself, I tend to stick with heels below five inches to avoid this aspect.

The second is that heels are difficult to walk in and require training to become familiar with the change in balance and one's centre of gravity. The trick I have found is to walk with the calves, to use them to press down on the heel and then use the hamstring to pull from the toe. This motion provides a forward propulsion that helps stabilise you as you walk. At least, that is what I have found. So, when I am walking in stilettos, I have the internal mantra of *Heel-Toe. Heel-Toe.* You have to trust your balance and go for it. Almost like riding a bike. If you slow down, the more likely you are to fall.

But if you manage to keep yourself upright and moving forward with confidence, they can really get the hips working, as well as shape your posture to throw back your shoulders and accentuate your chest.

And that, as succinctly as I can manage, is the basics of speaking and moving when presenting as female. Together with the previous few chapters, this covers the more logistical portion of the series. I know it is not the most glamorous or insightful information, but they are small details that are often overlooked when considering the transition. I hope they have been helpful to those who might need a few pointers to get them started on their road, or for those who want to gain a greater appreciation of what their loved ones might be going through just to live a normal, indistinct life.

This is the secret torment of the transition. It takes years of practice to become invisible, and a lifetime of maintenance to reach consistently the most base level of your desired gender's expectation. And if you trip but for a moment, there is no telling how far you might fall.

Chapter Seven

Sex, Exercise and Relationships

One of the reasons why I felt so much doubt and distress when dressing alone in my room was that I did not know to what extent it mattered. Was this a change or was I merely doing it for the thrill? There was certainly a lot of sexual arousal viewing myself in this light. Perhaps it was the novelty, the enactment of what was viewed as a social taboo, or perhaps it was unlocking in me intrinsically, pent-up urges that had not yet had a mechanism for their release. And while I can give no definite answer, and it will certainly differ from person to person, this is a point I wanted to raise here. The distinction is worth discussing because some may want to cheapen the necessity of the transition to life and livelihood by reducing it to nothing more than a mere kink.

However, it is prudent to say that not everyone is interested in sex. For them, there may be other subtle issues with which to contend, or maybe they can be spared one of the more tangled aspects of the transition. But for those who are sexually active, I know it caused me no shortage of confusion when I began to dress in more overtly feminine garb only to feel autoerotic sexual arousal when I saw my own reflection.

This sensation is called fetishistic transvestism. I raise it here because it can be difficult to distinguish from the euphoria felt when resolving or dispelling one's gender dysphoria. The sexual arousal at wearing the clothes of the opposite gender to one's assigned identity and the euphoria experienced when expressing one's truly desired identity occupies common ground. I am unsure whether the two are linked at a more fundamental level if one presides over the other, or whether they are ultimately separate yet share a similar state of mind.

Having the possibility that I was dressing for no other reason but the thrill, to live out some as-of-yet unforeseen sexual fantasy did not help. It was confusing. I was having an immediate physiological response to what I was doing, as though that was the clear and obvious answer. And it felt good. It felt right. I loved the way I looked when I dressed up, and I still do, especially if it is in the more overt affair, such as cocktail dresses or lacy camisoles.

But was this it?

Was I going through all these secret nightly interrogations, these doubts and lonely parades just because it excited me because it stirred some fantasy I did not know I had wanted? Was this the mask of someone else, some sordid performer to distract me from how inadequate I felt? Was I diminishing the grand question of one's identity but enjoying a quick splash of sexual pleasure? It was as though I was covering the hole I had found with the excitement of a new experience, one that felt right and enticing but which left behind the same person when the sensation had faded. The same person with the same abyss in their heart.

I was struggling at this point with the question of my sexual orientation. At eighteen, I thought I was bisexual. At nineteen, homosexual. And then, at twenty… what even was this? Was there really nothing more to this question than sex?

Except it was an unsatisfying answer. It did not resolve any of what I was feeling and instead only provided more problems for me to face. If this was a matter of sex, then why was gender factoring into it? Why did I need such tactile stimuli? And why, when the bubbling arousal had faded away, did I still feel incomplete?

I am writing this now several years on. It remains difficult to untangle the two or to recall the absolute reasons for my arousal and resultant shame. Yet these years have given me a vast array of new experiences. I have explored the realm of sex in multiple ways, both pretransition, during, and post, over a period of nearly a decade. With that surety tied now in my memory, it is less about the shock or the thrill of dressing or seeing myself in an autoerotic fashion, and instead, it is more about the feeling that I am finally living. It is one more avenue in which I can explore life the way I want.

Even now, I experience the same echo of autoerotic sensations when I see myself dolled up for the night or when I am engaging in amorous activities, but it is not for their position as fantasies to spice up what was for me a half-life, but because they are facets and validation of my gender expression. I am able to live them and enjoy them because I am able to live and enjoy them as my chosen gender.

The piece of advice I followed to get me here is that, as hard as it can sometimes be to separate the two, sexual orientation and gender identity are completely different things, but they can often disguise as one another. The gender as which I decide to live holds no bearing on those to whom I am attracted or that which I find sexually pleasant.

The question I then had to ask myself was: Why did I feel this way? Why cannot I gain any sexual pleasure unless I am presenting as female? I believe it comes down to the fact that sexual desire is not something we can choose. We like what we like. If we cannot explore that which we enjoy because we do not have the form of life to accommodate it, then we find no enjoyment in what we are expected to like.

I was living as the wrong gender and was trying to fit the typical image of the cisgender heterosexual male. This doomed attempt made me depressed, anxious, and inadequate when I failed time and again to reach what was expected of me. But I can now live life the way I want, with sex as but one more part of that life.

My desires, rather than a source of shame for being contrary to what I am 'supposed' to want, are now in line with the form in which I am best able to attain and experience them. Thus, what was triggered in me as a freak sexual arousal was, in hindsight, my body's way of telling me that there was a contradiction in my mind and a clue as to the direction of its resolution. I have given myself the green light to freely explore and experiment, so why would I not feel excitement at the thought? And if sex is a part of a dull life, how could I then enjoy it?

Because for many, sex is a part of life, and the transition is the transformation needed to experience life freely and without obstacles. It then follows that there is a crossover where one would feed into the other, stimulating what previously lay dormant. I guess what I am trying to say is to not be put off or feel shame over any sexual impulses you may get while dressing. It is a natural part of the process. Use it as a form of validation, a way to question yourself, to find the extent to which all this affects you and guide you to why there is this disconnect in your life. It could well be that for you it is sexual arousal for the sake of pleasure in a life already full and satisfying, in which case, I am glad you have found what works for you and makes you happy. But it is not a definite be-all and end-all state of affairs. Dressing may not be a way of only gaining sexual pleasure but could be a lighthouse to something far more fundamental.

The search it inspires can be lifechanging.

Sex may also be a part of a relationship you have, and when you are transgender, both have their quirks that are important to keep in mind. The individual method and manner of sex is best left up to each person to discover and enjoy. The only advice I will give is to have an open channel of communication between yourself and any partner where you can state any boundaries or requirements you want to be respected. Sex is a normal part of life and the more openly it is discussed the easier and less awkward it becomes as a topic between people in a relationship, and a lot of the problems it can present, especially for a transgender person, can be resolved by sitting down and talking about it.

On the whole, however, relationships have some subtle trickery that can make things difficult and feed the insidious voice in your mind that does nothing but want to make you doubt yourself.

Before the transition, I was single and had been for a while. I had relationships in the past, but they never lasted longer than a few months, most likely because I was not a complete person and therefore could not give myself to the partnership in the way that was necessary to make it sustainable. I was acting here too, and when the performance wore thin, it frayed until it eventually broke and once more cast me adrift.

So, I intentionally kept away from any relationship until I was at the tail end of the hormone stage. Not only did I want to be one-hundred percent comfortable in myself, or that I was going to be experiencing a number of tough years, but I was also scared – scared of coming out to someone as transgender in a relationship and how that dynamic might work. It was new, and untested and, due to society's and the media's often unflattering depiction of transgender people, I thought myself as inherently undatable and unlovable. Why put myself forward if I was just going to get hurt and rejected?

And this is the main difficulty when starting a relationship when you are transgender: the constant rejection. I have been passed over as an option for this fact multiple times, both implicitly and explicitly, on dating apps, in person, by friends, and by strangers. If I were cis, I imagine I would have had no issues getting myself a partner, but this single aspect acts as a filter and prevents a large proportion of people from even wanting to try a relationship. Unfortunately, this is not something you can control, and it will hurt. It will never stop hurting. You can only keep yourself moving and wait for someone open-minded to come along. They will see you for the wonder that you are, not despite the fact you are transgender, but because of it.

The transition enables so much personal growth and internal inquisition and helps unveil the true hidden depth of a person. What emerges is someone extraordinary for the challenge and transformation they have been through, and too many people cannot see past the physical to what beauty lies within. But this is the sad state of dating while you are transgender, and perhaps will be for the foreseeable future.

The second difficulty is something I have dealt with keenly over recent years, and this is the venom that is imposter syndrome. Perhaps my greatest fear is that of inadequacy, and being transgender in a relationship unhelpfully brings that in spades.

For the last few years, I have been part of a polyamorous relationship, with varying numbers of partners myself, many of whom have, or have had, other partners as well. Most of these were, or are, cis women and present me with a never-ending mirror for my own insecurities. Whenever I am alone, the snake spits at me and burrows as deep as it can go. It hisses at me, telling me that of course, my partner would like to spend time with his other girlfriends because they are 'real women'. They can give him what I cannot. What am I compared to them? I am but a hollow imitation, with my own set of limitations that prevent me from being all I want to be, the girlfriend I wish I could be.

This played almost on a loop during the first few coronavirus lockdowns. I was separated from my partner by social distancing measures, but he was not from the partner with whom he lived. I felt left out, cast aside. Once again passed over for the fact I am transgender.

These feelings came at a time when life was presenting me with almost insurmountable obstacles. This recurring mantra drove me towards the edge. At several points, I considered self-harm and suicide. Thankfully, I was able to recognise my proximity and seek help. I spoke openly with my partner about my difficulties and requested they not mention their other partners, while I returned home to my family. I disconnected from the world to recentre and recharge, away from the source of these feelings.

And while I have wanted to find myself a girlfriend, I have hesitated for similar reasons. I have been terrified that I would constantly compare myself to their cis femininity and find myself wanting. A cheap, misshapen image when held up against their natural beauty. Warped, malformed and half made up. Forever incomplete and unlovable as a result. Because why would anyone want to be with me when they could choose any cis woman and have all that I aspire to be but know I will never fully reach?

I have not found a single one-and-done way to stop these voices and thoughts, but I have found ways to endure them. Mostly I try to trust my own sense of self, my own brand of beauty because I know I bring aspects to a relationship by being transgender that a cis woman could not, and if someone wishes to reject me for that reason alone then it is their loss. I have so much more to offer than my gender and it is their fault for not being able to see beyond it rather than mine for not meeting some socially derived standard of acceptability.

Because it is a false equivalence I have in mind. We are all unique. And I am unique because I am transgender. It is part of what makes me who I am, coupled with my humour, hobbies, intelligence and self-regard, many of which have been altered and augmented by the transition itself. Without this, I might not be half the person I am now and perhaps less appealing as a result. And for those that accept me, they find a wealth of a person below the surface, and I have learned to open my vault to them and share in the vast intertwining of life.

While I might fear loneliness just as keenly now I know what it is like to go without it, nothing can take away from those times when I am connected to someone for whom I care deeply and know that they care just as much. Because we are both unique, having found what we were searching for in the other. And because everyone can offer something different, I should not compare myself to others because what a partner might find in them has no bearing on what I bring to the table. We are all there just to be happy and be with the people we love.

However, the snake continues its journey, and when my defences are lowered for one reason or another, it finds a way to sink its teeth a little deeper. The above, while not an immutable shield against its poison, at least gives me something to wield and endure until I make myself whole again.

I am hoping that in time I will be in a better position to survive the trial of a relationship without this constant inner struggle. I do not want to live with such doubts crowding in on me, but it may be that they are an inevitable part of seeking love while transgender in a cis-oriented society. But whatever happens, I know who I am. I am simply doing my best to get there, to meet people openly and honestly, the good and the bad, so we can create a more secure coupling, a lasting growing together.

For anyone feeling particularly lonely during all this, there will be something out the other end, a place where you can give yourself fully to another person and be accepted for the unique individual that you are. Beautiful because of who you are not despite it. And this is something worth reaching, for all that you do not know it will be.

Maybe then this helps those relationships that are already in place when the transition begins. If you can wade through the doubtful looks in the mirror, the wanting comparisons, the grief of losing the one you loved, the regret of whether you ever knew them in the first place, to the joy of discovering the vastness of the person yet untold and unexplored, and you find that you can love all that just as fervently, then that will be a relationship built upon a surer foundation. But in that same light, if a relationship does not survive, then would it have lasted come the other side? Would it have lasted in a life unfulfilled? It will be painful either way, but my last word would be to not grieve what has been left behind. Instead, be thankful that each step has happened and carried you now into the unpredictable trove of the future. If sex is a part of life, then change, to me, is all of life. And change begins with honesty.

Though there is little about the transition that comes easily or naturally. Every step is its own version of a struggle, either against yourself, against those around you, or against society at large. For this reason, there is a very real risk of mental health issues developing in transgender people, leading to an increased prevalence of self-harm and suicide. I am not an expert in how to deal with these matters, so I would encourage anyone feeling such a way to seek help immediately. Even though it might sometimes seem like it, you do not have to go through this alone. There are always people out there who want to do their best for you and ensure that you are healthy and happy.

I have sought therapy several times during my transition but have not found it the right answer for me. I am too self-analytical and know everything they can say before they say it. So, instead, I surround myself with a support network of close friends and partners in whom I can confide, who are there to catch me when I fall, but who also challenge my assumptions and counteract the poison my mind can occasionally feed itself.

The greatest obstacle I have found throughout the transition is maintaining my own internal balance, to keep from letting my emotions direct me to places I would rather not go. To aid in this, I started exercising a lot more. At first, it was to do with my physical appearance and hope that it would resolve some of my issues around confidence and inadequacy, but in time this routine became critical to my continued mental well-being. Because a healthy body helps foster a healthy mind.

The constant improvement, the weekly successes, and the surge of endorphins are all little victories that make me feel good about myself. It is not a lone solution, but it does its part, and I would recommend anyone who can to take up exercise as part of their arsenal of weapons against mental health issues.

That being said, however, exercising as a transgender person is not straightforward. Like much else, it has been fixated on the binary extremes – the ultra-sexualised feminine gymgoers as seen on TV, or the sculpted masculine bodies displayed on billboards and Hollywood movie screens. Not only do these deter one from starting for the impossibility of what is expected, but the roles are so clearly defined that it is difficult to exercise outside of them.

I was terrified of going outside for a run in women's clothes for this reason. Before I came out, I went to the gym regularly and went running a couple of times a week. But at first, I was scared to do either. In those days, I needed my make-up to present. I was paranoid that I would sweat it off, or that in body-hugging leggings and tops, it would be easier to tell me apart from other cisgender joggers, or the breast forms I wore would plop out part way through the park.

And yet, as with anything – and I guess this is a universal feeling – I did not want to lose what I had gained, even if it was just being generally healthy.

But there are solutions to this.

There are plenty of online exercise programmes and workout apps that focus on indoor, calisthenic routines. All you need is a soft mat and perhaps a resistance band, and you can do all you need to do without having to go outside. For cardio workouts, I purchased myself a fold-away exercise bike that I set-up in the lounge and ride for an hour or more several times a week. This has definitely helped keep me focused and centred during the long months of lockdown, over which much of my later transition took place.

There was a time when I craved the outside air while I exercised, so I tried running again. It took several months to build up the confidence, but in the end, I managed it by looping in several friends who also wanted to start jogging. We all went together, and having company made it a lot easier to break the ice. Though the compact did not last, it was an idea that had its potential and could be something to try if you want to continue running during the transition, or if you know someone who may be scared about going outside in such a context.

The only thing to keep in mind is to be aware that your physiology will change with the introduction of hormone replacement therapy if you decide to go this route. I will discuss this in more detail in a later chapter, but if you want to facilitate a physical change from male to female, shock and weight training, especially around the arms and shoulders, may not be the best direction to take. General cardio and callisthenics are ideal, as they can be targeted to train the heart, lungs and individual muscle groups, such as the legs, core and glutes.

Another thing they can work on is posture. I slouched when I was young, exacerbated when I grew quickly to my current height of 5'9" at the age of sixteen, which made me awkward and unsure of the extent of my frame. However, since coming out, I have found that I instinctively hold myself higher. I think part of it comes from a pervading sense of self-improvement, but another comes from the fact that holding my shoulders back makes them look smaller, as well as accentuating my chest. By straightening, I get a better curve for my back, meaning skirts and dresses sit more naturally. Exercising then the legs, glutes and core helps this foundation of my posture and is something else you can aim to improve upon during any workout.

The above areas are those that hormones will affect most directly by changing where fat is deposited, and by neglecting the shoulders they lose their stereotypically 'masculine' shape. Hormones will help here as well, as they do decrease muscle mass in the upper body, aiding with dresses and shoulderless tops.

Due to my years at the gym before transitioning, I had broad shoulders that appealed when presenting as male but were my mortal enemy when I switched to presenting as female. It took several years for them to shrink in size, partially limited by my bone structure – which, for me, is thankfully rather slender – but at the start, they were something I hid at all costs. I am only now gaining the confidence to have them out more, and it is freeing to feel positive about more aspects of my body as time goes on.

Your relationship with your own body, mind and any partners takes time to establish, understand and nurture. It takes effort, willpower, insight, experimentation and an open line of communication, but even though there are challenges to every aspect of life when transitioning, there are also solutions that can pave the way to a better future, and a fully realised 'you'.

Chapter Eight

Red's Choice

Throughout the years of my transition, I have had a lot of time to think about the various aspects of the change, its logic, and its consequences. I have been my own questioner, my own prisoner, my own salvation, and yet some things still remain a mystery to me. Why should gender be part of the equation? Why does changing my name, dressing and presenting every day and having every facet of my life coiled around this decision give me such control? Why does it make me so happy?

The problem is that as much as I have dwelt on this question, as much time as I have spent discussing it with friends and family, I have never been able to come up with a satisfactory answer. When I first sat down to write the series of blogs that eventually became this book, I was listless in front of my computer. I spent two hours trying desperately to come up with an answer. Midnight tolled, and the page was still blank. It is hard to distil the reason why changing my gender should instil me with such vigour, because it does not give me one single thing; rather, it gives me all of life.

So, instead of talking about what being transgender gives me, I will talk about what it is like not having it. A proof by contradiction, as it were. If it is good enough to determine that the square root of two is irrational, then it should be enough for me to prove the irrational reasons behind gender, emotions, and the defining change of a lifetime.

And this proof comes wrapped up in a story.

I was at my cousin's wedding a number of years ago, at this small country farm, and a wide gamut of the family was there. Because of this, it was 'suggested' that I present as male for the occasion. Many of them did not know about my situation and members of the older generations were going to be there. We were cautious about letting them know in the midst of a day that was not mine on which to impose. Also, there is the somewhat founded notion that those less familiar with the diversity of the modern youth can find it more difficult to accept such changes.

With my parents being major contributors organisationally, I did not want to add another mountain of worry to an already stressful day. While I agree that it was perhaps the most sensible course of action and that it could serve as a kind of last hurrah for my male presentation, it was distressing more than I can adequately describe. I was forced back inside an old skin and seen by people who accepted it, not knowing I was anything else, not knowing I was anything more.

Donning a suit, I arrived to little fanfare and the expected social routines. Being out in the country, there was not any reliable internet, meaning I could not hide on Facebook or e-mails from work. I was hounded by the laughter of mingling chatter from a crowd of people I did not know, and amongst all this, I was not sure who I was supposed to be. Who was I? Was I only what they were seeing, the awkward guy in an ill-fitting suit, or did the real me beneath all this remain valid even though it was stifled, confined, and roundly dismissed?

I did not want anyone to get close. Why give them the wrong impression? Why show them the mask when I knew it to be comprised of a decade of manufactured falsehoods? Why should I let my influence on others be limited to such a social character, a construct? It would be then like I was not there, but a scripted version made for such events, remembered as such by others and therefore nothing else besides.

Seeing as I was only going to be there for ten or so hours, it did not seem worth the trouble of coming out to one new group of people after another. Regardless of my bravado, it is almost impossible to silence the constant fear and doubt and remain staunch before another's imagined opinion of you, especially when the gain is so lacking compared to the trial itself.

I stayed in corners, kept my head down, fingernails scraping the inside of my pockets, gnawing at my tongue and the corners of my mouth, wondering if anyone would miss me if I stepped out and disappeared into the forest for a while.

Even though I knew they would, I still wanted to run. I thought it better to be on my own than bottled up again. I was a spider trapped in limbo, unable to demonstrate the fullest part of me, and yet unable to renounce the made up mutant I performed. And wearing a suit again for the first time in over two years… it was like wriggling inside a cereal box, one slowly filling with dirt, and suffocating. I was being buried alive. I only managed to make it through because those family members that did know took me aside to offer their support and a chance for me to breathe the real me. Even the groom. And for that, I am eternally thankful. But before long, I was chucked back into the fray, and this was exemplified in no better way than with the ceremonial photographs.

Weddings are an awfully traditional time, and the photos are no exception. We were on these steps leading down to the farm's grass courtyard and they wanted the family to gather around the bride and groom. Female members were to take the bottom step, male members the second.

Except… except, where do I go?

On that day, at that moment, I was presenting as male. I was seen as male. I was even being addressed by my old, male name, but inside I was squirming to get out and make a statement that what they saw was not accurate. But there was no step 1.5. No 'Platform 9¾'. There was only one step or another. So, I stood on step number two, and I hated myself for it.

My life was once again lived at the behest of others. All I could think about was the forest, about disappearing somewhere I could be myself, even if I was alone. Because, at that moment, it felt better to be on my own as me than let continue this clawing façade. If the limit of our identity is only what we are to others and what we enable them to become, then in both I would not exist in any meaningful sense. But at least in one I would be true to myself, rather than hiding the better part of me to ease the play for others.

When night came, I took refuge in those lonely stars I know so well and waited out the rest of the event as best I could.

There was a disconnect between the mental and physical, and regardless of my determination, inputs from the latter influenced the former. All my progress and insight became nothing more than nice theories upon which I was unable to act. I folded too neatly into conformity. What I am expected to be by others. What I expect of myself. I wanted to please those that saw me, even if it meant compromising who I was. I could not erase more than twenty years of this routine and the effect it had had on me, but I could use it as a steppingstone onto something new, the warning that I needed to align the internal and the external and make good on all my victories.

Perhaps then... perhaps this is as close as I can get to any form of an answer. Why is day-to-day living such a necessity for me? Because without seeing my new name on a letter in the post, without being able to try on a new dress every once in a while, without being able to fiddle with my earrings in the supermarket queue, I become just another lonely point of light, another face in the photo, and I slowly fade, until it was like I was never there in the first place. I become part of the parade others make of life, living what they give me so they can have their power and certainty. I conform to their world view. I sacrifice my identity so they can maintain theirs.

But I am aware I am no longer fine on the outside. I cannot maintain this façade. I must disappoint. Because although I have my flaws, I may stumble and fall, but I will also succeed. And they will be mine, and whatever they lead to will be mine. What I impart onto others in creating this communal story we all share will be mine. And I know that whatever happens, like this, I have the chance now to 'get busy living'.

The everyday has become easier in time, to hold back the fears of judgement and ridicule and to simply relish the fact that I exist. I have practised my craft, and just as any musician, actor or writer uses their skill to create the tools of their identity and to make an impact for the time that they have lived, so too does being transgender give me the same opportunity for self-expression. Take away the singer's voice, the actor's empathy, the writer's words, and you are left with no one. A shell. A non-being. And for me, clothes, make-up, hair, hormones and surgery… a name – they are my instruments. They are how I make my own step 1.5.

Now, this was where the chapter was supposed to end, and in an ideal world, it would. It represents a culmination of sorts. Sadly, though, life is rarely so neat and there are no true finales. A long time has passed since I first wrote this chapter as the blog entry as which it existed in its initial iteration, and I have had a lot of time to think about it. While the reasoning and the conclusion remain true, its sense of finality has fractured in the intervening years.

Even though being transgender gives me the chance to live in all its angles and definitions, that does not mean that occasionally I wish that I was not transgender. This is not enough for me to want to undo it all, everything I have been and done, but more to say that I wish I had not had to suffer, and continue to suffer, just to get access to the cis version of life. What they get by default, I have wounded myself and been wounded in the attempt, as if to show my worthiness for it. I must constantly play the social gender game, maintain myself to a set standard, and despair when, for reasons beyond my control, I fall short.

I wish that this was not the case. I wish that being transgender did not make life so complicated or intermittently painful. I wish it did not place demands and limitations on me. I wish things were simpler. And part of me does occasionally fantasise about what it would be like if I were not transgender.

Would I be happier? Would I have understood all that this book outlines? Would I inevitably go down the same road again? And if I had been born a cis woman, would I feel the same sense of regret over the years I never got to live, the classic experiences on which I have missed out and those I will never get the chance to know? And would every day be another battlefield to endure? Is being transgender a good or a bad thing for me? I guess my answer would orient depending on my mood.

What I am trying to say in my own rambling way, is that for all the answers I have found, all that I have achieved and all the growing I have done, I have not yet reached an end. I likely never will. I have not been made and finalised. There is a gap in my heart between the life I want to live and the life I can live, between the love I want to have and the love I can have, between the person I want to be and the person I can be, between how I want to look and how I can look, and I mourn that still. And part of that grief is occasionally wishing away the reason it is there. Wishing away the relentless burden of my gender.

Chapter Nine

Seeking Referral

What often goes unseen in the transition is the silent work an individual does for themselves before even coming out, and certainly before committing to a long-term change in any official capacity. When news and media covers or depicts transgender people, it is often done in reference to their medical transition, as though that gives it a certain validity it would not have otherwise. But there are years of work to even get to this point, as we have chronicled so far in this book. What the world sees as the first step of the journey is, in truth, an act of confirmation taken only after months of turnings and false starts.

However, now that we have reached that point and you are ready to commit to the medical side of the transition, the next few chapters will be dedicated to the more official and bureaucratic side of the transition process. Though, as a note, this will only apply to the UK's current system through the NHS as that is what I have personal experience using. Going through private medical treatment by using a private clinic, such as GenderCare, will follow the same broad steps, but the increased speed will also come with a corresponding price tag. Either way, you will first want to seek referral from your GP to a gender clinic, such as the NHS Gender Identity Clinic (GIC) due to feelings of intense gender dysphoria.

This is a daunting moment when everything kicks off and becomes 'official', in its own way. I was terrified about taking this step. It would change everything about my life, and how I interacted with friends and family and put a road of obstacles in my way. I would also have to open myself up to and talk about a sensitive subject when, at that point in time, I was too used to the act to risk being vulnerable. It was a weakness in my eyes, admitting to a problem and upsetting the image upon which my life depended.

I was scared of losing the little stability I had found.

But I needed to do it. I could not put it into words on the day, but still, I knew. I was being driven by a fundamental instinct, and I just had to trust that if I followed it, I would end up happy. Because I knew that to ignore it would be a slow but eventual desolation. To help, I brought a friend to sit with me in the GP's waiting room.

If you have any sympathetic friends, I would recommend doing the same. It is an intimidating prospect to tackle alone. There is a great sense of uncertainty here. The fears and doubts I have done my best to explain come to the fore, stronger than ever. There is a peril in embarking on something new and perhaps irreversible.

Is this really for me? What are they going to say? What if they refuse me? Would they be right to? And if they accept me, what will I need to go through? So much needs to be done now. How will people react? How will I tell them that this change will now become permanent? Do I want that? Do I need it? Will they judge me for it? Am I a freak to want this? What if I turned back now?

And so on.

A cacophony formed under your own spotlight.

But it is important to remember that this is your journey, and this is just one more step on the path to your destination, wherever that may be. At every turn, the professionals you will meet and the people you love will only want you to be happy, to want what is best for you. They will support you and aid you in reaching that place and you need only go as far as makes you most comfortable. There is no single way to be transgender and no single way to go through the transition. While there may be a common path, this is yours to make and take as you will. Trust yourself. No one knows better the true depths of you.

Heading to your GP and requesting referral may be the first instance of a concrete declaration outside an immediate social circle and can feel like a point of no return, a fifteen-minute chat after which everything changes. But this is not the case. While it does begin the whole process, it is nonetheless a slow process. It can, therefore, feel almost… anticlimactic in retrospect.

Because, in the immediate aftermath, not much will change. It will take several months for the referral to reach the clinic and for a reply to return, and then many years waiting for an appointment, at least with the current state of the system – thanks to decades of chronic underfunding from the government. And there may be several intermediary steps that can add an extra few months to all of this. The transition can accelerate with a short meeting with your GP, but you will have time to adjust and mentally prepare for the coming changes as they occur slowly and disparately over a period of years.

I will go into this period of time more in the next chapter, the unfortunate truth of these perhaps wasted years, but when I was first questioning my gender, I was advised to begin the medical process early, even if I did not feel ready. At that time, it took about two years from referral to receive a first appointment and another year beyond that to get prescribed hormones. This timeline has since bloated further.

Even though it can be daunting, it may be prudent to get the ball rolling, as it were, and use the time between referral and your appointment to make your preparations. You could use it to become more assured in how your lifestyle might change and look, make any administrative alterations to your name and personal details, or use the time to decide whether or not the transition is for you. I cannot speak for every person's situation and it is perfectly valid to express your gender as you wish, and this may not be in the form of a medically assisted transition. In which case, if you want to double back at any point, a phone call to either your GP or the gender clinic is all it takes. It is far easier to drop out than to get in.

And while the timeline will not be the same for everyone, this is how I advise viewing this part of the journey.

I prepared myself mentally during my time between. I got more used to dressing day-to-day, came out to my family, got a job, found somewhere to live, and piece-by-piece built the support structure I would need around me during the coming years. I did not know what the future held, but I did know that it was going to be the first few years of the rest of my life. And for that, the readiness is all.

Now, in more detail, the actual process of seeking a referral is done through your local GP. You will need to get an appointment through whatever means they have established, be that in person or through an online form or through a requested call back. Once you are speaking to your GP, you will want to ask to be referred to the gender identity clinic (GIC). The clinic to which you will most likely be referred is situated in London, near Finchley Road Station. This is The Tavistock and Portman NHS Foundation Trust Gender Dysphoria Clinic for Adults. There are also several other clinics around the country, and some specifically for children, which I will outline in a dedicated section in a later chapter.

Your GP will ask you to talk about what has led you to this decision, so it is wise to bring notes that lay out clearly what you have experienced, your thought process, and how all this has made you feel. This acts almost as evidence of your intent.

It is not the most considerate stance, but it takes a lot of resources to facilitate a transition and it is a permanent change for a person. For that reason, despite how it is presented in the news as something someone can just wander into, your GP and every professional along your path will want to ensure this is the correct decision for you, and that you will benefit from the transition. For that, you will need to convince them.

Even after years on hormones, I was still asked by members of the clinic to provide evidence that I was living and working under my chosen name. It may feel intrusive or insensitive not to take you at face value, but that is the state of the system. To get the best result you will need to play by its rules.

If you are under eighteen, you will need the consent of a parent or guardian and you will be referred to a different clinic, The Tavistock and Portman NHS Foundation Trust Gender Identity Development Service (GIDS) for children and young people, though this will be replaced in spring 2023 by a series of regional institutions to restructure and reinvigorate the level of care offered. These deal with child and pre-teen referrals as the medical process is slightly different due to puberty blockers. I will explain this more in a future chapter as it requires its own section of discussion.

The only thing to note is that due to extensive waiting lists, which are available to view on their website, there can arise a distressing situation that by the time you would receive your first appointment at the children's clinic, you would have waited so long that you would be over eighteen, in which case you would no longer be applicable for their process. While you may miss out on the medical benefits, they should honour your original referral date should you need to be re-referred to the adult clinic. This is another reason why it can be important to enquire sooner rather than later.

After discussing this with your GP and explaining the extent to which you are experiencing gender dysphoria, and maybe talking about the series of events that led you to this decision, you will together fill out a referral form that will go to the GIC with all the information they need to know. You can download this form from the GIC website and bring it to the GP yourself. However, this may not be sent off straight away, but can instead be held until after you have seen a psychiatrist to vet your referral and discuss more in depth what you are feeling and thinking. At least, this is what happened to me.

Thankfully, I found my assigned psychiatrist experienced and understanding. He told me that he saw people going through this process about once a month, and he knew the questions to unlock the trickier aspects of gender dysphoria. Even if, in the end, the full transition is not something you wish to undertake, it may be worth going through this step to understand it yourself and to talk it through with someone knowledgeable and impartial. Or you may explore private counsel instead. As with so much of the transition, the choice is up to you.

After this point, I would recommend keeping in contact with your GP's referrals department and chasing them about once a month for an update. After the meeting with the psychiatrist, I received a letter saying that he had approved my referral and I thought it was all done. However, after several months of not hearing any form of confirmation from the GIC itself, I double-checked with my GP and it turned out they had not actually sent anything off.

I am not sure why this happened. Maybe he needed my continued interest as a sign of confirmation, but that choice on his part put another five months onto an already extensive timeline. So, as soon as you receive approval from the psychiatrist, get on your GP and demand the referral form be sent to the GIC. Within a few weeks, you should receive a confirmation package with several forms you will need to sign and send back.

The GIC has an ongoing problem of people not turning up to their appointments, and wasting what little resources they have to spare, so they require a signed consent form stating that you are going to attend and that if you do not, you are kicked out and will need to re-refer. This may have changed by the time you seek a referral, but this was what I received back in 2016/17 when I went through this part of the process.

Once you have sent off this consent form, the waiting begins. It may be worth checking up with the GIC every now and again, either by letter or by phone. Due to their limited resources, the GIC, at the time of writing, does not have an interactive online presence beyond their website, so contact is done either by post or by phone. Post is the most reliable way I have found. Most of the time, when I tried to call, it went to answerphone or pre-recorded messages and I was left unanswered or without the promised call back. They can sometimes get in contact via e-mail to arrange online appointments and confirm contact details, but these are only done once you are in their system and more for administrative purposes rather than answering queries.

For me, it was more by chance and good fortune than competent administration that I learned of the date of my first appointment. I managed to get through to a human being rather than a recorded message and asked how my referral was going. It was here that I was told the date, though you should receive a confirmation by post several weeks or months before the appointment itself. I would therefore recommend making it a monthly or bimonthly routine to get in contact with the GIC to keep tabs on things. You may even get lucky and get an earlier slot because a previous person decided to cancel.

This is also a good life lesson for any part of the transition. Do not trust things to happen for you. You will need to take an active part in the administration process to ensure it all goes to plan. Be a nuisance and the job tends to get done. At least, that has been the case from my personal experience, pestering a variety of unfortunate receptionists.

That, in a nutshell, is the process of seeking a referral. The form itself that you and your GP will fill out is thorough and in depth, though it can get personal at times. It will ask about your sexual activities, libido, and your ideas towards gamete storage, which I will discuss more in the future. But all this information will be confidential and only used to help you in the end. The most important thing to keep in mind is that nothing's set in stone. You are allowed to change your mind. You are allowed to re-examine yourself and your feelings and this whole situation. The people at the GIC are understanding and aware of this. They will double-check your responses and talk through the outcomes of every option before going forward. No decision is made until you give consent and they are sure it is in your best interest.

While it may feel terrifying, that moment when you walk into the GP's to first seek referral, remember that it is under your control. You own the speed at which you take the process and the final say of whether you wish to undergo it or not. The very act of seeking referral becomes the formation inside of which you can begin to build your life the way you want to have it. Rather than seeing it as an occasion when you shed off responsibility to bureaucracy and outside influence, it is more an act of determination and the realisation of your newfound agency.

This may be difficult, as I know it was not in my nature to make such a splash. I was, and to an extent still am, a person who likes to take things as they come rather than risk rocking the boat. I like routine and find comfort in the familiar. I feared bearing the consequences of whatever happened next, but this is a moment when you must do just that. It is up to you, but I promise that in this instance at least, the assurance and maturity you must show to undergo something so difficult and life-changing will help shape things into how they were always meant to be.

The years that follow, as you wait to be seen, will be a time when you can act upon this growth and become ever surer in yourself. Each new day is an exercise in control over your life. As such, the outcome you reach, in whatever form it takes, will be fulfilling, defining, and glorious.

Chapter Ten

The Wasted Years

I wrote the first draft of these words on the 1st of February 2022.

At this time, on the GIC website, they state that they are currently offering first appointments for those whose referrals were submitted in November 2017. This is a difference of fifty-one months. Four and a quarter years. And with our government's current lack of dedication towards funding transgender care and the NHS as a whole, and with the growing awareness and social acceptance of transgender people, who are thus more likely to come forward seeking treatment, this disparity will only get worse. So, for those who are not yet on the waiting list, you face the daunting prospect of being forced to wait years for treatment or pay the price for private care. This is a gruelling choice by any measure, but this time does not need to be wasted.

For that reason, I wanted to write about what you could do to fill this time and use it best to your advantage. So, the title of this chapter is ironic in a way, but also, in a sombre sense, very much not.

The most common misconception I see from the public at large, and especially our lawmakers, is that the transition is something so simple and easy to fall into. With such lasting consequences, they believe it is necessary to protect people from going through it by accident or when it is not in their best interest. For that reason, the barrier to entry has, over time, only ever become more difficult to traverse.

I first felt this misinformation precipitated when I was a child being exposed to the idea of the 'sex-change operation', permeated as it was through popular media. I did not know then just how inaccurate and damaging that phrase was, as it gave the impression that you walked into the hospital one gender and got wheeled out another. As if that is all it takes.

Maybe that is why they fear and hate us. A transgender person might not conform to their idea of the world, and having a load of them running around unchecked distorts their picture of reality. Or maybe they are scared that it will happen to them or someone they love without due consideration, as though they have been converted by a social force into something they do not want. And perhaps this is why there is such contention around puberty blockers, parents are scared of their children being pulled into a process they do not understand before they are ready and without the necessary checks in place to ensure it is the right choice.

Either way, it is based upon the falsehood that the transition is easy, everyone welcomed without question and something just anyone can and would want to do. This could not be further from the truth. I hope, over this and the coming chapters, to utterly dispel that notion, because the outcome is that those people in desperate need of treatment are now no longer able to easily access the support they need and in despair might seek any other escape from the relentless dysphoria they feel.

However, the process, all told, can take anywhere from six to ten years, if you go through the NHS. The uncertainty comes from how lucky you are on the bureaucratic and administrative side of things and which set of medical changes you wish to undergo and how they affect you. The cost can vary depending on whether you pay for your prescriptions or not if you decide to pay for your own hair removal, and what surgeries you wish to undergo, as some of the more cosmetic operations are not covered under the NHS.

If you wish to go private, there are private gender clinics that are worth investigating, such as GenderCare. In this case, it is worth checking the medical staff. Those that work for the NHS can sometimes also run or work in private clinics. These are going to be the most experience and dedicated. The timeline for private care drops to about two to five years, but the price can rise significantly even for the most basic treatment, and the initial cost will be much higher. I have seen many transgender people, unable to bear the lengthy wait for the NHS service, crowdfund from among their friends and the wider community to afford entry into the private sector.

This is the choice every transgender person must face. Do I pay to get the treatment I need? Do I wait years just to be seen because I cannot afford not to? Or do I do my best to get along as I am now, give up on the transition, and hope it does not get too much for me to bear?

The fact that you must add these extra, mandatory years to access the NHS course does make it a more daunting prospect than it otherwise should be. There will be this not-insubstantial period of time when it may feel like there is nothing you can do, days quite literally slipping away unlived. But as much as it may feel like it, these days do not need to go by having been wasted. They are an opportunity to take important personal steps and make ready for the changes yet to come.

That does not mean, however, that these days are going to be easy. The whole transition is, by definition, a time of change, but this is when that change will be most immediate and pronounced, and yet always coming too slowly. It is this time in-between that you will make the initial alterations needed to start amalgamating one life into the other, but while you may want to end one day as one gender and begin the next as the other, it is not so simple to allow such a rapid transformation. It is an effort of months, of steady steps towards a final result. Laying the foundations, changing your name, coming out to all the necessary places, getting the documentation ready, establishing your everyday appearance and trialling it in more quotidian social scenarios.

Yet, as much as you might relish the taste of this coming freedom, the possibility that all this is leading somewhere grand, there is still that shackle about your ankle. There will be those places that still have your old name. There will still be those occasions when you cannot yet present the way you wish. There will still be the looming knowledge that you have not yet started the medical transition. Should anyone peer too close, they might see through all your efforts and define you instead by everything you are not, rather than what you are trying desperately to present.

You do not exist as one or the other, but in the limbo between, dependent upon context. A constantly shifting mask based on the audience and what they expect to see. And knowing what freedom is like only makes it harder those times when you must revert. Out of habit. Out of necessity.

During this period, I was shackled by my old biology and as such, it was difficult to fully express myself and live life the way I wanted. As much as I desired to take charge of my life, show my agency, and impart my identity through my own version of the every day, I still had to conform to some social occasions, present as male for my hair removal treatments, and experience a swamping fear every time I went to the corner shop to pick up some bread.

Having even just one more year of this, in my case, was awful. Plain and simple. It pushed back the time when I could take the reins for myself and one less year I would have to enjoy the ride. I had already missed so much and spent so long as a spectre floating from expectation to expectation. I wanted to live, but I had to go through the motions, listing from day-to-day, a faded victim of an established routine. This is the subtle difference between surviving and living, with the transition being the key to opening the gateway from one to the other.

During this year, I made sure that every aspect of my life that was tied in any way to my gender transition was within my scope of organisation and I knew how each part of it lay. I became the master of my own life for the first time.

In this regard, I finished my university education, came out to those friends to whom I had not yet spoken, I told my family, I began researching in more detail the medical process and surgeries, and how I would go about changing my name and gender on paper. I also built a support structure around myself, personally and financially. I found somewhere to live with people I could trust and began the inroads into the world of employment.

I was unbelievably lucky that my first job allowed me to work from home as it made this period of time a lot easier to exploit. I will go into more detail in a later section, but I could maintain the assigned male work persona through a Skype window without having to worry about the commute or office life, and outside of this I could continue my own advancements, treatments, and experiments, with the two remaining completely separate.

I began saving portions of my paychecks to pay for the upcoming transition and any surprise costs that might arise. I knew there would be train tickets to London and back to get to the clinic, that my hormones would be on costed prescriptions, and that some cosmetic procedures would have to be done myself, such as my hair removal.

Most of all, however, that year was a period when I could experiment with dressing more day-to-day, starting the routine of doing so around the house, getting used to the idea of life like this, and eventually just… living a day.

I remember well my first full day presenting as a female. It was a trip down to the nearby high street. My local Sainsbury's was there, so I thought to merge this initial effort with a task that needed to be done anyway, my weekly shop, to keep me focused and moving forward. I had the plan to help lead me through. I also went up and down several of the charity shops there looking for clothes to expand my new and burgeoning wardrobe. Every step of the way I was supported by my housemates at the time. They flanked and guarded me, made sure I was safe but also that I would not retreat. This was a hard first step, but it needed to be taken for there to be more in the future.

And I built it up from here, day by day until each new day was full and mine. It took several months, and sometimes I would make myself ready to face the world only to turn back at the front door, or even my bedroom door, and curl up in fear and shame, wishing I had the strength to face this endless challenge. But over time, I managed it. These days I moulded to fit my purpose and I moulded myself to fit what these days demanded of me until it became an attainable routine. I could do more of what I wanted to fill the time, to make this life my own, including heading down to Sainsbury's all by myself to pick up my much-needed loaf of bread.

It took a while longer before I was able to extend this new-found certainty to the more official aspects of life, such as work. I will give being transgender in the workplace its own dedicated chapter as there is a lot to discuss on that topic, but for now, I will say that I was waiting until I had the authority of my first appointment behind me and the assurances of being a full employee, rather than still being in the easily-dismissed trial of probation. I did this to have as much legal and medical backing as possible so they would be forced to bow to the situation, change my details on their systems, and know what to expect from the timeline.

While I did not know exactly what would happen or when, with this routine and substance in place, I knew that whatever did occur with hormone therapy, and if I decided to undergo any surgeries, I had all the pieces in place to hold myself together, emotionally and administratively. The transition is a period of one threshold after another, each one more distant and uncertain than the last. But each is, in its own way, inevitable. And you must face them, deal with the consequences, or remain trapped behind the wall in your head.

My focus now that I had gathered together my own forces was to remain healthy and happy as I struggled through the coming typhoon of psychological and physiological changes. No matter what, it was under my control. I had instigated this. It was by my choice that my life had taken this direction, and each day that I lived with the goal of moving forward is one I was glad to have lived. I had gathered the strings and could pull on them how I wanted to make this time my own. These days were brighter for having such purpose; they served to grow me as a person. And whatever came, I was going to make of it the best I possibly could.

So, my advice for these years would be to get on the waiting list early, even if it might be before you are ready so that you can use the intervening time to make yourself so. After all, it is easier to call it all off than to get through the door in the first place. And if you realise it is not for you, or you find that the full medical transition is not how you wish to proceed in carving your own identity in this world, then you can call it off through a phone call or a letter.

But if you decide to go forwards, these years are crucial in preparing yourself emotionally, mentally, financially, and administratively. You can use it to get a support network around you of friends and family. You can update any accounts, consolidate the administration of your life, and sort out your living situation, education, and employment. You can change your name if you are at that point and amend any documentation, secure those aspects that need securing so that when the time comes every contingency is in place, and should things go against you, you still own the rest of your life and can continue moving forward.

Because the only thing you should need to worry about when you head through the door to your first clinic appointment is making the most of the chapters yet to come.

And they are good chapters indeed. Trust me on that.

Chapter Eleven

The Gender Identity Clinic

At times, it felt like an unreachable goal, a place of myth. Only the truly blessed or lucky were allowed to go, and only devotion and fortune would allow entry. It took me about three years to get to this point after coming out socially and about eighteen months after first requesting a referral. And this stature of inaccessibility has only grown in recent years, with the waiting list as long as it is. Some may never reach it, either because they do not believe it is worth it, or they simply cannot stand the wait. But for those that make it this far, we have finally reached the Gender Identity Clinic (GIC).

Depending on your age and location, there are currently eight gender clinics spread around England accessible through the NHS, and several more available privately. For the former, your GP will refer you to the most appropriate to your situation and location. You can go to the NHS website to learn their details or see the summary below.

London and the Southeast

The Tavistock and Portman NHS Foundation Trust, Gender Dysphoria Clinic for Adults.

Lief House
3 Sumpter House
Finchley Road
London
NW3 5HR

Phone: 020 8938 7590
E-mail: gic@nhs.net
Website: https://gic.nhs.uk/

The Tavistock and Portman NHS Foundation Trust Gender Identity Development Service (GIDS) for children and young people.

GIDS
The Tavistock Centre
120 Belsize Lane
London
NW3 5BA

Phone: 020 8938 2030
E-mail: gids@tavi-port.nhs.uk
Website: https://gids.nhs.uk/

Update: As of 28th July 2022, the GIDS service was earmarked to be shut down from spring 2023 due to criticisms from an independent review board, and regional institutions established around the country to take over the needs of young transgender people. Further details of these regional clinics have not yet been made available.

The North

The Tavistock and Portman NHS Foundation Trust Gender Identity Development Service (GIDS) for children and young people.

8 Park Square
Leeds
LS1 2LH

Phone: 0113 247 1955

Sheffield Health and Social Care NHS Foundation Trust Gender Dysphoria Service.

Porterbrook Clinic
Michael Carlisle Centre
75 Osborne Road
Sheffield
S11 9BF

Phone: 0114 271 6671

E-mail: porterbrook@shsc.nhs.uk
Website:
https://www.shsc.nhs.uk/services/gender-identity-clinic

Leeds and York Partnership NHS Foundation Trust Gender Dysphoria Service.

Management Suite
1st Floor
The Newsam Centre
Seacroft Hospital
York Road
Leeds
LS14 6WB

Phone: 0113 855 6346
E-mail: gid.lypft@nhs.net
Website:
https://www.leedsandyorkpft.nhs.uk/our-services/gender-identity-service/

Cumbria, Northumberland, Tyne and Wear NHS Foundation Trust Northern Region Gender Dysphoria Service.

Benfield House
Walkergate Park
Benfield Road

Newcastle
NE6 4PF

Phone: 0191 287 6130
E-mail: NRGDS@cntw.nhs.uk
Website:
https://www.cntw.nhs.uk/services/northern-region-gender-dysphoria-service-specialist-service-walkergate-park/

The Midlands

Northamptonshire Healthcare NHS Foundation Trust Gender Dysphoria Clinic.

Danetre Hospital
H Block
London Road
Daventry
Northamptonshire
NN11 4DY

Phone: 01327 708147
E-mail: genderclinic@nhft.nhs.uk
Website:
http://www.genderclinic.northants.nhs.uk/

Nottinghamshire Healthcare NHS Foundation Trust, The Nottingham Centre for Transgender Health.

12 Broad Street
Nottingham
NG1 3AL

Phone: 0115 876 0160
E-mail: not-tr.gender-services@nhs.net
Website:https://www.nottinghamshirehealthcare.nhs.uk/nottingham-centre-for-transgender-health

The Southwest

Devon Partnership NHS Trust West of England Specialist Gender Dysphoria Clinic

The Laurels
11-15 Dix's Field
Exeter
EX1 1QA

Phone: 01392 677 077
E-mail: dpn-tr.thelaurels@nhs.net
Website: https://www.dpt.nhs.uk/our-services/gender-identity

The one to which I was referred was the first on the list. It used to be located by the Charring Cross Hospital and was there for many years. For this reason, many in the community still refer to the London Clinic as the Charring

Cross Clinic. That was how I knew it and was where I went for my appointments, but it has now moved.

In a previous chapter, I covered how to contact them and how to seek a referral, so I will talk in this one about what it is like going there and what to expect when you arrive. Some changes may have been made since moving to their new offices, so bear in mind that not everything may be accurate to each individual's experience and how they are now established to meet and treat patients. Hopefully, though, it should provide the broad strokes idea and lessen the uncertainty over this next big step.

After first contacting my GP in August 2015, I finally arrived for my first appointment at the London Clinic during the spring of 2017. I was fortunate enough that my parents were up to the challenge of coming. From what I saw while I was there, this was not the case for everyone. Some had brought friends with them, while others had been forced to come alone. The difficulty for parents should not be underestimated. While we all wish that they would love and support us as their children regardless, they go through a transition too, of sorts, and for some going to the clinic with their child is a step too far and comes years too soon.

I recommend wherever possible, if your family is not up to the task, to have someone there at your side. As much as you may want and need the help of the clinic to go through the transition, it is a substantial obstacle to see through alone. This is a big moment in the transition, where the course is laid down and the wheels truly start to turn, and facing the prospect of that outcome and finally bidding farewell, in part, to the life that led you here, is terrifying. But for the actual consultation, this will take place over an hour-long conversation with one of the consultants there at the clinic.

For mine, we went over much of what I have covered so far in this book. They did challenge me, and made me prove to them that I had gender dysphoria and that the transition was what I truly needed. As I have mentioned before, they do not want people walking into the process that will not benefit from it and does not want to use their resources where it is not necessary, so they will interrogate you and ensure you meet their strict barriers to entry. It does hurt having to convince people over and over again that you are transgender and that you need this treatment, but this is how the system is set up, much as it is thought otherwise by the public, the media, and our lawmakers, and we must do our best to weather it for our own needs.

We also discussed what had led me to the decision that I needed to transition, the responses to my referral form and how they would be reflected in my course of treatment, the treatment options themselves and what their side effects would be, and lastly, a timeline of events. Most of these I have or will cover in their own separate chapters in more detail, but I received a summary booklet and checklist at the end of the consultation. It contained a substantial amount of crucial information that you should not need to wait years to receive and could be informative far earlier in the process. This, I will paraphrase below, augmenting it with my own experiences where appropriate.

Blood Tests

During the referral process, you may have your blood taken and the results sent to the clinic; however, due to the waiting list, they normally require a second batch taken more recently or they might even do it themselves at a nearby hospital. These tests are important for two main reasons and are continued throughout the early stages of your hormone treatment.

The first is because the hormones themselves can affect liver and kidney function, simply for the fact that you are giving your body more to filter than normal, and these tests are designed to check that they remain healthy throughout. The second is to first gather a baseline for your levels of testosterone and oestrogen and then to track this against their projected path during your treatment. I had routine blood tests for the first two years after receiving my hormones. The dosages were changed when the levels in my blood did not match what they wanted to see to get the desired results.

However, if they do take a baseline test during or just after your first appointment, they will draw a lot of blood. They did for me, as I imagine they had a lot of tests to run and things to check, and therefore needed many samples. They drew around six complete vials and I felt light-headed afterwards and unsteady on my feet. I would recommend taking some crisps, chocolate or an energy drink with you, so you can stock up on sugars afterwards. And also have a sit down just so you do not hurt yourself.

Psychology

Gender dysphoria is a challenging thing to comprehend. It comes from a place beyond logic and many experience depression, anxiety, and suicidal ideation as a result. This is something the clinic takes extremely seriously. As such, if they believe it necessary, they will offer access and referral to a system of specialist counsellors and psychiatrists. If you think you can benefit from this, I would recommend taking advantage of it. I did not, as my friends and family provided all the support I required, but from what meetings with counsellors I have had on this topic, they have been well-informed, compassionate, and are a good sounding board.

But what I will say is that once you undergo hormones, you may experience changes to your thought processes and emotional state. I will discuss it in more depth during the chapters on the hormone treatment itself but suffice it to say that I have found myself becoming more in tune with my emotions, less dependent on logic and reason, and sometimes carried along at their whim. This may be scary and could result in you needing someone to speak to about these changes. For me, they have played a part in a wider array of mental health issues, such as anxiety, depression, and post-trauma responses.

It is never a weakness to seek therapy should you feel that you could benefit from it. If it is recommended or you want to take this route, the option is there and provided for you through the clinic. Though, as with most things regarding the NHS and especially their gender services, there will be a waiting list, so factor that into your decision as well.

Speech and Language Therapy

I covered this in the chapter on voice, but I will expand here on the clinic's offerings. The GIC has their own team of speech and language therapists. Naturally, while they are seeking to expand their team due to the recent increased demand and the specialist knowledge required, they have a long waiting list. Yet, I was assured this was worth the wait.

Due to my proclivity for the theatre and my vocal experience in that regard, I did not choose to take the individual speech sessions but did elect to join a series of monthly group sessions. While the individual consultations focus more on discovering your own personal style and then training the voice to replicate it consistently and automatically, the group instead focuses on public speaking, giving presentations, and talking on the phone. These were areas with which I had been struggling and I hoped would give me the confidence to use my voice in a wider range of real-world situations, especially those that arise in a business environment.

Having been through these sessions, I can say that they were a success. While they did not dive into the techniques you can use to modify your voice, they were more a playground for putting your progress to the test, praising areas of strength, and constructively guiding those that could use improvement. Something that stood out to me while I was there was when they gave me a check sheet at the start for me to gauge my own confidence in my voice.

The questions it asked did probe into areas of weakness and provided me with a personal goal. At the end of the six-session course, they gave out another check sheet so you could mark the difference and the progress made. I was taken aback by how far I had come even in those few sessions and what they had done for my belief in how I could use my voice to enable and compliment my presentation.

Core Facial Hair Removal

I underwent this through a private cosmetic clinic in the months and years before my first appointment to get something done during the time spent waiting. I have also continued it past my time at the GIC, orchestrating it to my own needs and timetable.

If you go for facial hair removal through the NHS, it will be several months before you get your course started due to the volume of recipients and the funding hoops inherent in the system. While I did not get hair removal for my face, I did get some done in preparation for my gender confirmation surgery, which I ended up opting out of, but it did give me some insight into their process.

They only use electrolysis, and instead of having their own in-house specialists, outsource it to private clinics dotted around the country that are certified by the NHS. You are tasked to find the one closest to you and organise the treatments yourself. After examining you, they will apply for funding depending on how many sessions they think it will take, and only when that funding comes in can they begin.

This amount of paperwork can add months or more to the time spent waiting, and it may not get the results required. At least personally, I have had great difficulty in having the hair around my lips and chin removed via any method, so once the funding runs out, you may be left with some hair and no way to be rid of it. I found going through private salons gave me greater control over the organisation, duration, and speed of these treatments. Even though I have not reached total removal, and likely will not for a while, it enabled me to do enough soon enough that I could present day-to-day without the increased difficulty provided by the constant threat of coming stubble.

Gamete Storage

This is a more personal aspect that will differ based upon the individual, but it is recommended by the clinic before starting hormones as one of the side effects is infertility. You will be required to contact your local fertility clinic and do so through your own initiative and financial resources. Whether to go for storage or not is completely up to you and I cannot advise one way or the other. But it is one of those decisions in life where it may be better to have it and not need it, than need it and not have it.

I decided to store mine and found the workers at my local clinic understanding of my situation. They provided me with the necessary material and respected my gender and identity even though on paper it perhaps presented some anomalies. After taking the sample, they checked my sperm count and mobility.

I had been tucking to present for several years, having done so nearly all day every day. This had increased the temperature of my testicles for long periods of time and caused a noticeable drop in fertility, but not enough to render me sterile. There was enough there that should I wish to undergo surrogacy it would likely result in successful insemination. This is important to consider, because if you wait or have been tucking for a significant amount of time, you may not get the results you wish.

The overall cost of storage is around £400 per year. This pays for the liquid nitrogen they use in the freezing process. It may be different depending on what type of gamete is being stored, but I doubt the order of magnitude would change all that much. They do often offer bundle deals, where you can pay for several years at once at a discount, and at any time you can request the gametes are destroyed and payments stopped. Though this requires your signed consent to facilitate.

Smoking Cessation

6On this point, the clinic is very strict, expanding the criteria to encapsulate most recreational drugs. Some can render you ineligible for treatment if taken within a certain timeframe before attending the clinic. For smoking standard cigarettes, they give you a cutoff date of three months before your second appointment, when they would analyse your medical history and recommend the prescription of hormones.

Now, about that second appointment.
You should discuss possible times at the end of the initial consultation, and receive your date and confirmation letter several weeks later. This is where, all going well, the clinic consultant will write to your GP recommending they prescribe hormones. It will usually take a few weeks for the necessary paperwork to come through and to have the appointment with your GP to get the actual prescription.

Through the NHS, this second appointment takes place twelve to eighteen months after the first, though this may have increased since I went through the process. For me, my two appointments were ten months apart, from April 2017 – February 2018.

This is another one of those awful waiting periods and I did what I could to fill the time, already fully prepared for what came next. On top of continuing to grow my confidence and live every day as best as possible, one thing I did use the time to do was to change my name and title and come out at work.

I will go through each of these in its own chapter as there is a lot to discuss, but I will say that the GIC does not require you to have officially changed your name or gender by the time of your first appointment and you need not present as your preferred gender either. I did not when I first went as I was on standby for work and they did not know at this point. For your second appointment, however, they do require either your name changed in advance or for you to bring evidence of it to the consultation, and for you to present as your preferred gender.

To offer some perspective, from first seeking a referral to getting my hormones was about a thousand days for me. This will be much longer now due to the increased wait times for a first appointment, so expect it to be several years before you can get your hands on hormones if you go through the NHS. This might seem like an insurmountable amount of time, but keep in mind that you will have many more days than this to enjoy the fruits of the treatment.

Lastly, as a point of administration, when you go to the clinic and sign in at the receptionist's desk, they will give you a form with which you can update any contact information. I had moved between my referral and appointment and they had not received my letters stating this. Ask to take a few of these forms home with you. This is what you will need to send them, along with any name change documentation, if you are alerting them prior to your second appointment. Also, ask if you can get a way to contact your consultant directly, such as a work e-mail. They may say no, but you can always post letters to them, which I found to be the most reliable form of contact with the clinic. I used this when I needed my consultant's authority when it came to providing evidence to certain institutions that my name change was serious.

And that, as best as I can outline here, is all you will need to know about the GIC. I hope this has helped contextualise things and prepared you for what may come in the future.

Chapter Twelve

Changing Your Name

Names are the cornerstones of identity. They are the summation of who we are and how we declare ourselves to the world. They are the first concrete marker we have to announce our place in society, interact with its people and receive its benefits. And yet, when we are born, we are given a name before we have even had a chance to become the person that name will come to wholly capture.

For that reason, many who go through the transition and begin to uncover the person they are at their core will choose a new name that better represents this new version of themselves. In a way, we are all claimants for the names that become our statements, either by selection or embodiment. But there are two major topics on which to focus when discussing the changing of your name. The first is administrative and the second is emotional. I am going to tackle them in that order as the latter is more abstract and trickier to define, and my thoughts may not be universal; though they may, I hope, help clarify this part of the process.

Before I begin describing how I changed my name, there is a link to a transgender-related page on the UK's

Deed Poll Office website as well as a general FAQ page that covers in more detail some of the topics and questions that either I did not encounter or that did not apply to my situation. I would recommend looking through them for anything I do not cover here. You can find them as subsections to the Adult Deed Poll Information menu.

Now, all in all, it took me several months to traverse the complete name-changing process. This was mostly due to administrative delays and relying on the speed of the postal service, but in one respect, for a reason, I will get into later, it took a lot longer than that.

The thing about a name is that it is not legally binding. You can change your name at any time, the only condition being that you must alert every necessary institution of the change. If you intentionally withhold your change of name to escape some legal obligation, this can be penalised. Be sure to make a list of everywhere your details are held before you start, so you are ready to let them know as soon as you can.

As with most transgender people, I had an idea of the name I wanted to use long before I changed it officially. There are several ways you can change your name but the easiest by far is by free deed poll. There are several websites that allow you to create a deed poll document, either by supplying the wording for you to create the form yourself or by having you enter the necessary details so it can then draft it for you.

The most important aspect to note is to not go anywhere or use any service that charges for a deed poll.

Having it drawn up by a solicitor, ordering it from the UK Deed Poll Office or enrolling it does not make it any more or less official. A deed poll is merely a declaration that you are going to abandon your current name and instead go by your new one. It does not change your title, but titles, unless they are inherited, like Viscount, are not controlled by the government or any institution. They are yours to change as you wish on a case-by-case basis, though you may be limited to the titles available to be selected depending on the organisation to which it applies.

Using a website such as the one I described above, which is what I used myself, creates a form after you input the necessary information. This includes your new name, your old name, your address, and the details of two separate witnesses. Once this is done, I advise printing off a single copy and then meeting with those whom you choose to witness the signing.

Witnesses must be people with whom you are acquainted, but they cannot share the same last name as you – new or old – or live at your address. I chose friends I had met at university as my witnesses and we gathered one evening to do the signing. One even baked me a cake. I spent about fifteen minutes practising my new signature, wishing I had thought about this sooner. Even trying to make it different, without sufficient practice, was very much a relic of habit.

Once you and your chosen witnesses have signed the document, that moment is when your name is changed. Now, however, you need to let everyone know. I would then recommend getting between twenty and thirty photocopies. While I had some left over after sending off all those that were required, it is useful to have some spare just in case you need one several years down the line. For example, my deed poll was needed five years after first changing my name when it came to the process of receiving money from an inheritance.

There is a guide on the UK Deed Poll Office website that includes a list of the most important places to alert of your name change, though these are just the most common and will likely be augmented to each individual's situation.

I went through this guide and picked off those that applied, adding any others that needed to be there, such as magazine subscriptions and my GP, and made my list. I then wrote a mail merge letter introducing myself, stating my wish for my records to be changed, the reason why, and my full name and title, both new and old. I labelled them clearly in the centre of the page so there could be no mistakes. I also included a line saying that I was sending this to all necessary institutions and that if they needed more information from me, such as account numbers, they should write back.

With my deed poll and cover letter both now sorted, I bought a stack of envelopes and stamps, making a package for each institution that included both documents. I posted these over the next couple of weeks and most of them were successful, with confirmations returning within a few days. Some needed more information to identify me, but once they found me in their records the changes were made to both my name and title. Also, remember that when you are sending one of these packages to the GIC to include one of their own 'change of details' forms. You can pick several of these up from the clinic when you go there for your first consultation.

In some places, I could change my name online, through the site's support channel, changing your account details, or speaking to customer support via e-mail. It is worth checking each site to see if this is possible as it can save you some time. The only difficult online one was the Microsoft account that was linked to my Xbox profile. I made this with my old e-mail address when I was young and it included my old name. I could find no way to switch it over to my new e-mail address as all my data was linked to that old account. The solution I found was to log into my old account and change the e-mail alias to something new and set it as the default. While it would not change the e-mail address fundamentally, it would now show in most places as the new address, mitigating that issue.

There are three places, however, where the process is slightly different.

The first is your bank. Depending on which bank you are with, this may have to be done in person. I went to my local branch with a copy of my deed poll and cover letter and spoke to someone behind the desk and told them that I wanted to change my name. They brought out one of the managers, who had the authority to make such an alteration, and they took me to a station to do so. They were understanding about the fact that it was for a gender transition. The man who worked with me that day knew a transgender person himself and helped calm my nerves. After it was finished, they gave me a form confirming what had happened and several days later my new bank card arrived. However, for some reason, they were unable to change my middle name, but as this is only an initial on the card, it did not affect me too much.

I am with two banks, and the second was slightly different. They could not make the change in-branch so asked me to write a declaration of the change to go off with my deed poll. I said I had already made one, the cover letter, and they used that instead. The behind-the-scenes process took a bit longer, but my card arrived just fine and now my details are changed at both of my banks. For them, I presented as male when I went into the branch and they accepted it – there was no requirement that you must present as your preferred gender if you are not at a stage when you are ready to do so. It is certainly a stressful enough moment as it is.

The second place is the DVLA. They require a secondary, corroborating piece of identification to confirm the change, namely a passport. This is the reason why the process for me took a little longer than I initially made out.

The passport office, the third institution, are more careful in their process and not only need the deed poll form but passport, valid photographs and a letter from the gender identity clinic confirming that you are transitioning and that it will be a determined, long-term change. I would recommend asking for a letter from your consultant during your first appointment.

The reason I did not change my passport until I was at the stage of everyday living was because of the need for updated photographs. I had not started hormones when I first changed my name. This would come just under a year later. I knew they were going to change how I looked in subtle ways that would coalesce to create my new image. I wanted to wait until after I had been on hormones for long enough for the bulk of these changes to occur before I committed myself to the evidence of printer ink.

But when I was, I had my photos taken, filled out a passport application form from my local post office, and took these along with my deed poll, cover letter and the letter from the GIC to the passport office in London. I had an appointment booked and spoke with someone behind the desk who made the change for me. At this point, I was presenting as female for everyday life, but I doubt there would have been an issue otherwise. It seemed like another day for them and the change was made with little opposition or fanfare. Within a week, my new passport had arrived.

Two further notes are that most websites, such as commercial sites, let you change your name at any time through their online portals and accounts. You can do that whenever you want to get a head start on the process.

And lastly, there is something called a Gender Recognition Certificate (GRC), which is a government-issued document that enables retroactive name and title change for similarly official documents, like birth certificates, and for getting married under your new gender. This costs £140 and requires proof of living as your preferred gender for two years. There are plans to lower this barrier to entry, which have been passed in Scotland, but at the time of writing they have not yet gone through in England, and the government has not only reneged on its promise to reform the system but is attempting to block the Scottish bill, thereby scapegoating transgender people and putting them at the heart of a constitutional debate.

Unless you want to make the change complete both forwards and backwards, I would recommend skipping this document. It is an extra step that presents a lot of administrative challenges with little day-to-day application or reward. I am living comfortably and am employed without having an issued GRC in my name.

However, be aware that I did encounter a problem where, without an updated passport, when applying for a new job they were required to input my details on their HR system to link with the HMRC using the name and gender displayed on my old passport. I will go into this in more detail later, but to have the correct gender displayed without an updated passport requires a GRC. This may change if the process is ever reformed, but that does not look likely to happen anytime soon.

Now that we have the administrative process out of the way, I will talk briefly about some of the emotions I felt during this whole period. The most pervading sense was, counter-intuitively, one of anticlimax. I chose the name Lucy after a character I created in one of my early attempts at writing a novel.

While the book itself did not turn out the way I wanted, the name always resonated with me, the sense of freedom that the character sought, their defiance and their wish to regain control. For that reason, I used the name from the day I came out, and when it came time to make it official nearly two years down the line, it was not a moment of change but more one of confirmation. I was already sure, and all that was left was a signature to convince everyone else.

Yet I still do find it strange, even today, when I hear my new name used out loud. It takes a lot to overcome decades of expectation and habit, and I still turn if I hear my old name used, even if it is just a stranger speaking about someone else. But changing my name got me a sense of control. I never anticipated this, but the sheer amount of administration it took almost enforced it. When you consolidate your bank details, your finances, your savings, and your accounts for any subscriptions, it becomes yours more now than it ever was before. It goes back to what I said about the transition being one of finally living life to the fullest. This is one element of that. It is yours now. You make it yours. In name now as well as in deed.

But changing your name does not only affect you. While your friends, I sincerely hope, will be accepting, they may need some time to get it right, for which you will need patience and love. From my experience, the difficulty comes with the family.

A lot of the grief my family experienced during my transition stemmed from the use of names. I compromised and only changed my first name and first middle name, leaving the heritage of my familial and ancestral middle names intact. This way, socially, I can choose how I identify, but for all official purposes, I am still a member of my family.

Yet, even with that in mind, for years after changing my name, they struggled to even cross the threshold. Instead, they called me by the moniker of 'L', as both new and old names begin with this letter, and compromised by using gender-neutral pronouns. They feared they were losing the child they had named and loved for over twenty years. I did my best to explain that the transition was an extension, not a replacement, but they still needed time.

It is a common factor, I have found, within as well as without the whole transgender experience, that names hold a certain power. The personality of their arbiter is wrapped up in the name itself. We are given our names before we even have the chance to become our own person. We,, therefore, grow into our names. This, however, I believe, has some faults. If you were to swap the classification of rock and table, it would not change their internal structure; they would still be used for the same purpose. All that would change would be their entries in the dictionary.

To the same effect, while my name might have changed on paper, I am still the same person, except now

I can grow to fit my new name because it is the identity I have chosen. It represents me better than what was first assigned when I did not yet even exist.

When I was at school, I shared my name with two other people in my year and they were as far from me as you could get. Where I was a conscientious student, one was a hazer, apathetic to a fault, and the other was an outright bully. It was hard to believe that we shared the same name. But this is an extension of personification, how we attribute humanity to inhuman things, such as pets, teddy bears, items and objects. With a name, we imprint upon these labels facets either of ourselves or, especially in pets, ones that are recognisably human. The name then takes on the amorphous property of identity, one seemingly linked to the owner of that name.

But changing the name does not discredit the time that has been lived; instead, it gives a chance for self-definition. Personality does not change with the alteration of a label, it evolves naturally over the course of a life. Beneath the limiting nature of a rigidly applied label, identity is made through experience and connections, memories and mistakes. All my old traits are still there, applied now to my new name, but with the freedom granted to me by the transition, I can now shape myself from here on out. I can influence and be remembered for what I become, not for what I was made.

This is the reason why I felt my name change day was anticlimactic. It was not a declaration of anything I did not already know. It did not change anything. It was only a barrier to entry I was more than ready to meet. For nearly two years I had used my current name and unveiled the personality that had always been there, one simply imprisoned by old expectations. I was not becoming anyone new or being reborn in any way – I was just confirming that this was me and the person I would continue to be.

It may be that I would not be the same person I am at this moment had I not gone through the transition, but that desire for expression would always have been there. It would just have taken longer to emerge, and I would be looking back at a lot more than twenty unfulfilled years.

Before we close, this chapter is a good place to talk about the title I chose for this book.

There are so many aspects of life that are defined around a person's name. It is the first meeting in work, family, and relationships, in every online account and passing social interaction. It is the entry-point into life. All this changed because I changed my name. I am loved by my name. I am hated by my name. I can love by my name. I feel loss by my name. I am happy, I am sad, I am accepted and discriminated against, and I can dream and explore, examine and engage by my name. Call me by my name and I can live life by my name. I am made whole by my name.

It is only a singular aspect of the transition, as we know by it occupying but a lone chapter of this book, yet it is nonetheless a singularity around which everything else orbits and by which they are made possible. I am not the definitions or expectations placed upon me, nor will I live at their behest. I have done all this by my name. It is the sum, the word that encapsulates me and with which I can finally enter into life.

When my family were struggling, centred around the idea of using a new name and how they were losing the person they had always known, this is what I learned: they were not losing me. I was not changing in any way more drastic than the natural evolution and blooming of a person over time. A name does not mean anything. It is what you do with it. It is merely a statement of intent. And I intend to live free and revealed.

Chapter Thirteen
The Corporate World

The content for this chapter comes from a speech I gave during a seminar that discussed what it was like to live as a transgender person in the corporate space. For that reason, there may be some overlap with topics discussed elsewhere in this book, but the focus here will be solely on being transgender in the workplace.

Because it is a daunting and terrifying place. The consequences, obligations, and expectations placed upon you in such an environment demand conformity where the transition is, by its nature, a bucking of social trends. Add to that the fact that the office occupies a large proportion of one's life, and it will never be easy to escape such a space with the way it has been built and continues to operate, but there are ways to navigate it and prepare yourself for its shortcomings. Hopefully, then, my history in this world can illuminate this underappreciated yet no less encompassing part of the transition.

When I came to give this speech, and indeed write most of this book, I was once again struck by the looseness of memory, daunted by the vast, near unrecognisable distances I have travelled and how many the minute steps were to get here. I can barely remember these past eight years, less so the person I was before. It has become my life. How then can I catalogue the infinite spectrum of moments that have built immeasurably to the present?

As I have stated, I first came out socially in 2014, near the end of my university career, and then began the medical transition in late 2015 by seeking a referral to the Gender Identity Clinic. Due to the waiting list, I knew I would need to enter work using my male name and presentation, as I had not yet reached the stage of identifying as female every day. I would only then come out once all the necessary pieces were in place.

So, for the first six to eight months, I was known to this company by my old name and identity, and I had to grit my teeth and go along with it. I played the part within their gaze and left everything else for afterwards because I was terrified of what they might say when I did come out.

I knew I had the law on my side with the Gender Equality Act, but there are ways to get around it. I have seen and heard of others, who should be protected against discrimination, with their neck under the knife for any wrong move, any justification to allow their employers to get rid of them. This has happened to members of the community and those suffering from mental health issues and mental illness. Would it be the same for me? And should I be spared this, it does not even account for the interpersonal relationships that would change between myself, my manager, and my colleagues, when the announcement was finally made. Would they accept me, or would I be a pariah, contractually obliged to my office-bound exile?

My parents had me hold out until the end of my probationary period. In case they were not accommodating, being a full employee brings certain benefits and assurances. But I was fortunate that my first job allowed me to work from home, which immediately discounted many of the stresses I had initially feared, such as commuting, office life, and long hours trapped in a presentation that was not truly mine. I could be me at work because I could curate the image they expected to see through a Skype for Business window. Meanwhile, outside of this, I could continue with my transition and keep the two worlds entirely separate.

That is, until 2017. That summer was when I changed my name by deed poll, as documented and outlined in the prior chapter. After the small ceremony, my friends threw for me and having received confirmation that I had passed my probation, I e-mailed my manager and the head of sales, who was perhaps the second or third most important person in the entire company. In as matter-of-fact manner as I could manage, I let them know of my situation. I included a copy of my deed poll, the expected timeline, any allowances I might need, and how things should continue normally regarding my work.

It was one of those e-mails that were so important and personal that I was petrified to press send. Nothing would be the same after it pinged into their inbox. I dissociated a little while I waited for their response.

Thankfully, I need not have feared. The head of sales called me up twenty minutes later to tell me that it changed nothing. He was glad I felt comfortable enough to come out. They would alert the team and make the changes through HR to my name and e-mail handle. He had just been scared I was e-mailing to resign!

After that, work-life continued through the Skype window, except I could present as myself. A few people did come forward to offer their congratulations and support, but for the most part, very little changed. Working from home allowed a distance from corporate life that offered a comfortable balance where one did not impact too much on the other. I was just a name and a profile picture churning out work seventy-seven miles away. All that had changed were three letters in my name and my Skype avatar. I still did my work. I still got paid. The corporate relationship did not rely on my gender.

At least, only for the moment.

Like many, that job did not last forever. They made me redundant about a year after I came out. I was made to go into the London office to return my laptop and devices and was then shown the door. I remember calling my father, who also worked in London, needing someone to talk to. While I was standing in tears at the side of the road looking for a friend in a strange city that had just kicked me to the kerb, passers-by wolf-whistled and catcalled me, perused me with their eyes and admired a body in its first attempt at office attire. Even in the despair of sudden unemployment, I was keenly aware that whatever happened, I was entering a world that would not see me as I wished to be seen, but as I was expected to be seen. An object to be used for what satisfaction I could give others, be it visual or commercial.

But I had little choice. I entered the role of the job seeker.

I changed the name on my CV, remade accounts on all the major job boards and went about it as you normally would. For the most part, I got the same silence back as I had before. But when I was finally offered another job, I encountered the strange obstacle of HR and HMRC.

At this point, I was still waiting until I started hormones before updating my passport due to how the treatment would affect my appearance. Because I had not yet amended this single document, the name as which HR would know me and how they would refer that to HMRC was still my old name.

My deadname.

I tried my utmost to get this changed, battling with HR over a series of passionate e-mail chains, and while they could have my new name on my paychecks and on all relevant internal systems, at the heart of it my deadname would be the truer version to them. It was a terrible prospect. All my hard work over the years did not matter. This outdated version of myself was the more important, the more valid. It was not me. Words on paper overrode my desperate protestations. I understand the difficulties of operating within a strict legal framework when you do not conform to the expected binary settings, but that did not stop my tears.

Still, I worked. I joined the office having been forced to come out just to fight a battle I never could have won.

This second job did not last long at all, which was perhaps for the best, but that did not make it any less painful to endure. The main reason was that the commute was untenable, not just from a logistical stand point but also from a dysphoria one.

Something that is not considered much when it comes to the obstacles a transgender person might face in the office is the silent discrimination they encounter due to the foundational construction of our society. Not all harassment is intentional, visible or malicious. Some occur from the looks and offhand comments you get when you fall outside 'the normal'.

The commute and the phone call are two areas where these are brought to the fore.

Just going outside can be scary.

There is the inherent uncertainty of whether you will be welcomed or whether you will be hurt for being who you are. Every step is a battle against a social doctrine, and it does not take punches to bruise you. Words and looks work just as well. And being forced every day to try your presentation in a train crowded with grumpy strangers, under the interrogation of halogen bulbs, against the backdrop of the expected 'office image' is a trial that is almost impossible not to fear.

It took me years to not have to work up the courage just to get on a train or a bus, and even longer than to not squirm beneath the voiceless onslaught.

Every journey is a performance, every carriage lamp a spotlight, and every crowded platform an audience. And just one bad review can set you back a long way.

And the phone is equally daunting. During the group sessions I had with a vocal coach, discussed during the chapter on the voice, and there was a whole section dedicated to speaking on the phone. Vocal dysphoria is one of the hardest aspects to overcome.

The voice is so tangibly linked to your physiology and identity that it can be hard to change and maintain without thinking you sound foolish in the attempt. With a history in acting, I had the luck of knowing the techniques to alter my voice and to be used to it sounding strange to my ears, but that did not make me immune to the terror of the phone-line gauntlet. With only my voice to act in my defence, how would I be received? Would I be called 'sir' or 'madame'? If I said my name was Lucy, would they believe me? Or would they be silent in confusion? Even now I am not that great at phone calls because of this uncertainty, because I cannot always trust my voice to not give the game away, as it were. Every word must be perfect. Every time. And that is hard.

Sometimes, it is easier not to try.

But life went on and I joined another office. This time I had my paperwork and my passport all in order. Finally, I could start a job without having to come out just to get through the administrative door. Looking back while I write this, I can only laugh at my naiveté. I had not contended with the next obstacle in a seemingly endless parade of hardships.

My hormone treatment, which I started in the spring of 2018.

Hormones change you physically. Would my colleagues, who I would sit near for eight hours a day every day for months really not notice when I began to alter right before their eyes? I kept myself under the radar for as long as I could. I even used a holiday abroad, and the two-week absence, to stop using my breast forms so that when I returned, perhaps they would have forgotten what I had looked like before I left. Luckily, they did not notice when I shrunk several cup sizes. But I could not hide forever.

There are so many appointments and medical treatments involved in the transition, of which HR needs proof to put into their system, that you cannot keep your head down for long. You have to say why you need to head to the hospital and why your clinic session needs an entire day because the nearest gender clinic is in London and they put the appointment during work hours because it is the only spot they had free, and you cannot miss it otherwise they will kick you out and you will have to start all over again.

So, I told HR. I had to. But I did not tell anyone else. I could not face the trial of coming out all over again to another group of people who I would probably not know for all that long in the grand scheme of my life. Why put myself out there? Why put myself at risk for so little benefit? And this team, this office's culture, did not inspire confidence in me that I would even be accepted should I do so.

I worked in sales at the time and the stereotype is true. It is a boy's club. As the only woman at the table at times, I was the one who was tasked to get the teas and coffees, do the sandwich runs, clean the office and prepare the conference rooms. I was supposed to write bid documents, but instead, I was buying bananas at Asda so they could have a fruit platter for their guests. I was called 'chick' and 'bird' and watched as others were too. I was taken back to that phone call to my father on a London high street, crying as people hollered me for my gender, when I was reprimanded for my outfits and made to feel ashamed of my body. Using the same reasoning to excuse rape culture and female objectification, they blamed me, the victim, when I could be seen by others as a sexual object. When I complained, when I cried before them, they pushed me aside and threatened my position. And when I took this to my parents, hoping for support, they shrugged and said that was the way the world worked. They said it was my fault, and that they had seen it happen too. To me, they were complicit in their apathy.

All because I was seen as a woman.

I was just trying my best to live my own version of every day and get on with my work, but I was made to feel lesser and different. This is not just an obstacle for transgender people, but for all women, and now I was in the firing line as well.

Maybe I felt it more keenly because I was newer to this life than someone who had grown from birth to expect this kind of unfortunate attitude, but it was still a challenge not to let it get the better of me. I did not succeed. I cried at work. I wept before my manager and the HR officer who made me feel like an object and reviled because of it. And when it was all over, to keep my job, I put on my mask once more. Just as I had before I came out, I became who they wanted to see, and in the background, I searched for another job. For an escape.

I had to get out.

Finally, I found myself at a company that allowed me to be myself, voice my experiences, inspire a culture of acceptance, and even have help supported by company policy. But before I could discover this side to them, I kept the same routine as I had before – head down and do not rock the boat. It was not worth the risk or the effort. Do your job, get paid, go home, and live your life elsewhere.

But work becomes so much of your day that it is hard to wear a mask for so long, to hide yourself away month after month. Eventually, I came out because I felt like I needed to. This was not for my own benefit, but for the greater benefit of the community as a whole. I came out because I needed to make a call to action against the government's decision to restrict puberty blockers to young transgender people, which would only cause harm and the eventual suicide of those who saw no other course.

I needed to use my voice, my position, my experience, even should it come to my own detriment, even should I need to weather another time coming out to another group of people, because it needed to be done. And what they never tell you is that you do not come out just once. You do it every day to every new person in every new way, and it is never not a question of risk. Risking change for truth.

Thankfully, I was accepted.

Almost immediately afterwards I was directed by my manager to the company's policies on the matter. They offered accommodation and time off for any medical treatments, surgeries and post-operation recovery. There was gender-based discrimination mentioned throughout, and company-wide e-mails from senior management mentioned diversity, making special note of those in the transgender community. There was even an LGBT+ and transgender flag by the front door to the office.

All this was truly great to see. It helped inspire a culture of acceptance and not one where I felt the need to cry behind a veil just to get through the day.

This brought me to the point when I could say all I have written in this chapter to a group of my colleagues during a work seminar. And I did so for the same reason I am writing this book. I speak my own personal torment because it needs to be heard. It needs to be understood by everyone, including those outside the transgender community. The details need to be known so the discussion can be had. Only then can we create a more accommodating world for transgender people, corporate or otherwise. I do not want them to have to go through what I went through just to live their own version of the everyday.

In the early days of the transition, I just wanted to get on and live my life without interference and without needing to stand on a pedestal and take on the role of a preacher, a presider, a defender.

But I long ago gave up on that idea. I have been forced to live instead as a representative of the community because we are not there yet. I must put myself forward to make things better for others. I must sacrifice my own privacy, my own dignity and history, and undo the dream of a life lived just for me because I will not be complicit in my apathy.

It is why I am here. It is why I out myself to interject and correct others when I am out in the world. It is why, with Hunting Hearts, my transgender rock band, I stand on stage, a guitar in hand and shout out the fact that I am transgender. Because there will be generations after me that will not have to face these obstacles. There will be generations that will know they are not alone from the first day of their journey. And while progress is being made, sadly, they will have to wait a little longer.

Chapter Fourteen

Hormone Treatment

To write this book, I had to do a lot of soul-searching, a lot of things to sort out in my head: emotions, reasons, my failings, and even the more basic matter of figuring out dates and timelines. But one thing that struck me was just how long a process it has been, and my journey went smoothly. Now, due to increased waiting lists, it is impossibly longer.

I remember first seeking a referral in August 2015. It was around the same time I went to perform at the Edinburgh Fringe Festival. I even found a less-than-favourable review of our show to confirm the date. I went to my second consultation at the GIC, the time when I was to be referred for my hormone treatment, in February 2018. I actually received the medicine itself in May 2018. That is a difference of thirty-three months.

Or just over one thousand days.

In the chapter on the Wasted Years, I wrote about how to fill and make the best of the time that is paid in performance to the transition process. While I did give advice about coming out to any remaining parties, organising yourself in preparation, and living as best you can as your preferred gender to get into the habit, looking back at those thirty-three lost months, I am split about how I feel about them. Is it a happy nostalgia for how far I have come, or grief at how much fuller that time could have been lived were I not subject to this inefficient process?

I do not think there is any individual solution beyond that of a complete systematic overhaul and investment to decrease waiting times. But for those who have already paid the toll, who are stuck on the ferry, slowly freezing in Cocytus's dead waters, there is no way to convince the ferryman to get that time repaid.

I wept when I first wrote these words. No great tears, just a gentle mourning. How much have I missed? How many small interactions and subtle moments? The tropes of youth and teenage years. The comfortable family unit. I was given a late start to a game everyone else had so far enjoyed, and by remnants of my biology and the years already spent, I am limited in how much of it I can now aspire to experience.

I fear I will become a victim of my logarithmic brain. If you track the years of your life with each taking a proportional fraction of the total, then the middle of your life, with an average span of around seventy-five years, occurs in your early twenties. I was twenty-four when I started hormones. Was I past halfway? Had I missed out on the best moments I could have had due to a quirk in my brain, a misplaced gender, and a faulty system that was meant to help?

There is no way I can tell. I will never know the outcomes of the 'What if'? inquiries and I know it is fruitless to think of them, but it is impossible not to contemplate the happy days I could have had. The pain comes in recollection. Those one thousand days are gone in a struggling click of a finger, unfulfilled and unexplored. The years that preceded them, not knowing the full person I could have been, contain moments and memories I never got the chance to experience. Precious days without my unique mark upon them, and even now I am still not through. Perhaps I never will be.

I have failed and I have been failed.

I guess the only solace I can give myself is to realise that while memory might well be logarithmic, time itself is linear. One second upon one second. Relentless. Come to the end of all this, living life as me and on my terms, I will finally have had the chance to fill them, as much as I could, with novel and interesting experiences and make each second stick perfectly in my imperfect mind.

But before I get there, there is the turmoil of hormones. It is natural to be scared. My first puberty was eight years of hell. To me, I feared hormones would be a 'round two' for which I was not ready. Being someone who likes predictability, coming face-to-face with a complete unknown was terrifying. I could not picture a life beyond that second appointment in February 2018. And yet my fear was overridden by my impatience. I was a greyhound in the slips, waiting for the off.

So, what could I expect?

I will touch on here the general physical changes of the hormone treatment, but the entire second part of this book will cover in more detail the step-by-step process my body and mind underwent. Due to the nature of this change, I will be forced to discuss elements of anatomy and biology some may find discrete or distressing. However, I will speak as forthrightly as I can for two reasons. The first is to dispel the aura of mystery and uncertainty that lingers around the body of a transgender person. And the second is to educate those who are on the cusp of their own transition about what they are likely to experience. This is so they need not fear it as much and can decide whether such changes are best for them.

This book is primarily from the perspective of someone who was assigned male at birth and transitioning to identify as a female. For that reason, it will be this avenue of hormone treatment that I will discuss in detail.

For those transitioning to identify as male after being assigned female at birth, I recommend searching the internet for similar oases of knowledge. I would be surprised if there are not several reservoirs out there for you to find. The only hurdle you may encounter is that many sites limit photographs that are considered pornographic, and as those people documenting their transition may do so by taking pictures of more private body parts to illuminate s the expected changes, these can be forcibly removed. I know many who once used them as a crucial source of insight and information only to now go without.

Instead, I will use words, to the best of my ability, rather than images, and I sincerely hope you find them useful. What I include in this chapter is based on the notes I was given during my second appointment at GIC. While I will give as much detail as I can, I will not give the names or dosages of the medicines in question. They should be prescribed by a doctor based on your biology and blood tests, as there can be unintended side effects if not properly managed, such as blood clots and kidney and liver failure. I do not want anyone reading this to use it as a replacement and hunt out medicine for themselves outside the approved channels due to the danger involved.

I nonetheless advise you to research the expected changes in your situation. Hormones affect everyone differently. There are as many transitions as there are transgender people who go through them. You may well have a different journey to mine and experience things I have not and could not cover here.

This book should be but one part of your readiness.

An Overview

Hormone replacement therapy (HRT) primarily uses a daily dose of oestrogen tablets, often in conjunction with a testosterone blocker injected into the muscle once every three months. The injection, for me at least, is done into the muscle at the top of the bottom, just below where it meets the hip and the small of the back.

The combination of these will cause infertility, which is why gamete storage beforehand is recommended by GIC consultants. Hormones are only recommended after being seen by two consultants, psychiatrists or psychologists to ensure it is the correct treatment. Some of the changes are irreversible and they wish to be sure that it will not cause you harm, or that you are not doubting whether it is the treatment you want.

Before you start, and then regularly while on the treatment, blood tests are taken to make sure that dosages are correct and that your hormone levels fall within the expected range when compared to your baseline. They will also be used to check that your organs are responding in a healthy way and not working too hard to filter out these new chemicals. The kidneys and liver are of the most concern. Also, as oestrogen thickens the blood, they will educate you on how to be aware of any clots, which will mainly occur in the lower legs or thighs.

Due to this, there is an expected increased risk of deep vein thrombosis (DVT). Studies have found it to be higher than the public average, but the clinics are aware of this. Should you experience any tenderness or swelling in the legs, you are advised to go to the hospital immediately and alert them of the treatment you are on so you can receive the appropriate care.

Alternatives to oestrogen, for those who react badly to the treatment, and experiencing nausea or headaches, are available.

Your dose of oestrogen is likely to increase after the first three months of therapy. The idea is not to push too much into your system too quickly. Puberty takes time, and this treatment aims to mimic that process. Also, the body can only handle so much taken via tablets. Patches are sometimes issued if the required dose exceeds a certain level, as this deposits it directly into the blood rather than going through the digestive system first.

The testosterone blocker itself overstimulates the pituitary gland in the brain that controls the testicles. At first, this may cause an initial increase in libido before the gland shuts off entirely. A drug can be given for the first two weeks to counteract this sudden increase in libido if you find it distressing. For those over forty-five years old, this may not be as big a problem and the oestrogen on its own should be enough to control any urges.

Due to the overactivity in the pituitary gland, it can produce prolactin. This can cause the gland to grow and press on nerves affecting vision; however, when this was discussed with me, this side effect had only been reported twice in all the years of HRT and it did not warrant removal of treatment in either case.

To ensure that any side effects are caught and treated as needed, there are several blood tests done on a variety of bases. They will increase in frequency before and after any surgery, otherwise will wane over the years and as your body settles into its new routine.

Any treatment you are on stops temporarily six weeks prior and for two weeks after any gender confirmation surgery. This is done to prevent possible complications with deep vein thrombosis. If you undergo surgery and have your testicles removed, then the blocker injections stop. Without the testicles to create the hormone naturally in large quantities there is no longer a need to artificially suppress the levels in your body. Otherwise, and along with the tablets, these measures will be a lifelong commitment.

There are other effects, especially emotional and mental, many of which I will cover in more detail in the second part of this book. There may be other side effects I did not encounter, in which case it is prudent to do further research and consider if needed, access to a therapist. Some testosterone blockers can cause depression, and puberty is naturally a difficult time. This is no different for one brought on through artificial means. There will be mood-swings and subtle changes in your personality as the hormones balance themselves out.

What will follow are the general effects of HRT and all the information that was presented in the pamphlet given to me by the GIC. Hormones affect everyone differently and there is no way to predict the outcomes, as they are dependent upon age, ethnicity, genetics, general health, etcetera. So, I wish good luck to anyone about to undergo the treatment and pray the changes to come great and swift. It may seem scary, and it may be difficult, but there is now an end in sight, and the chance to live a better and fuller life as you. Implacably, uncontestably you.

Facial Hair

You will find that within short order your skin texture and tone will become smoother and softer, accompanied by an overall reduction in facial hair growth. The effect on the skin will take place over the entire body and both measures reach their maximum several months into treatment.

This will not be a complete eradication of facial hair, and will still require external intervention if not already done so, such as using those methods described in the relevant chapter earlier in this book, but the hairs will become softer and sparser over time. Even four years after starting my hormone treatment, I must still shave at least every other day to catch the last few stragglers who have survived the hair removal process so far. These are mostly gathered about the lips and chin. Yet, I will endeavour to be rid of them once and for all.

Also, male-pattern hair loss slows or stops completely within this same timeframe, but any hair already lost will not grow back.

Breast Development

Perhaps the most visible and desirable aspect of the hormone treatment, breast growth usually occurs within eighteen to twenty-four months of a cis-woman's puberty. The treatment aims to mimic this pattern.

The process will begin around two to three months into the treatment, but they will develop slowly over time.

I wore my breast forms for roughly a year following the start of my treatment. The maximum effect is reached after two to three years. You should expect to grow breasts around one cup size lower than your mother, as I was told by my consultant, as there is an element of genetic input here. My own breasts lie somewhere between an A and B cup, but on my frame, I find they look natural and work well for my figure.

Higher doses do not have any benefit and can cause irregular growth, and there is no external way outside of surgical intervention to improve or extend this growth. However, without mammary glands to provide support, breast growth is dependent solely upon the deposition of fat behind and around the nipples. If you are thin, this may limit their growth, so attaining a fuller, healthier weight may increase breast size.

The majority of transgender women choose to undergo breast augmentation surgery in addition to this treatment. If you decide to go this route, it may be wise to start saving early. Considered a cosmetic operation, it will most likely not be covered under the NHS scheme. The usual cost at a private clinic sits in the £5,000-£6,000 range, with the possibility of other costs being applicable depending on your situation and for maintenance over time.

Some places may recommend a further drug to help increase breast growth; however, in studies, this has been found to lead towards a greater risk of heart attacks and breast cancer, so is warned away from by the GIC. There are, however, no published studies researching the risk of breast cancer in transgender women where this additional drug was not a factor.

Body Fat Distribution

Where fat is deposited is directed by your body's hormones. In the cis-male, it is mainly seen in the arms and the stomach. For a cis-woman, this changes to the breasts, the hips and the buttocks. The overall proportion of fat in your body will increase during treatment, with the majority going to the aforementioned locations, which will give a more rounded form to the body.

I started the process thin and angular; however, over the years, I have gained a subtle set of curves that I really like. They are not always visible, but certain outfits do highlight them and I am keen to have a body that I finally like. I also gained about a stone in weight since the start of my treatment, which is likely to have helped in this process. All of this has also been accompanied by a decrease in muscle mass in my arms and shoulders and a corresponding lack of upper body strength and definition. For me, though, this has been a celebrated loss and one I hastened through neglecting to exercise those areas.

Genital Effects

Before surgery, you can expect your testicles to become smaller and softer, and your libido and erections to decrease. Sperm production will slow and eventually stop. If you wish to store your sperm for use with a future partner or surrogate mother, this will be your last chance to do so. You will need to arrange this at a local fertility clinic as outlined in my chapter on the gender identity clinic.

It took about a year and a half to two years for my libido to return, and even then it did not do so to its pre-hormone levels. If sexual activity is a big part of your life, this may cause some despondency and distress, but for me, without the urge, I found that I did not miss what I no longer desired. Now, however, with the level having eventually stabilised, I have found that my libido is enough to enjoy sex frequently and pleasurably. It has not swayed too far in either direction, be it to wildness or impotency.

You may also find that the size of the penis will shrink slightly as the years go on, and for erections and orgasms to become less virile or reliable, either by being premature or entirely absent depending on the day. The change in penis size will not be eminently noticeable, but enough that the amount of skin available for future surgeries may become limited. If you decide to undergo gender confirmation surgery, they will examine you and determine if you require hair removal around the base of the shaft to allow for the future construction of a vagina. I will cover this in more detail in the final section of this book.

Puberty Blockers

The topic of puberty blockers has been in the news multiple times throughout recent years and has even made its way into the rhetoric of several high-ranking governmental personnel. For that reason, I wanted to give them their own section so they could be discussed to their fullest extent. While I have not had access to them myself, my proximity to the community has made me aware of their significance to those for whom they are an option and made me empathise with the threat they face without them.

For the content of this section, I have drawn from a closed letter I wrote to one of those government ministers in response to a speech they gave that touched on the matter of puberty blockers and my resistance to the opinions and potentially political decisions contained therein. I have of course edited it heavily to fit the tone and purpose of this book, but I wish for my original intent to be known because it is only through action that change can occur, and without it, things may change for the worse.

I may not be a certificate-wielding expert. I may not be a doctor. I may not be a politician. But I am a soldier on the ground. I have lived in the trenches for close to a decade and seen its horrors. I have heard its tales and felt the pain of those hurt and lost to the struggle. I have lived many of them myself.

And now I am reporting back.

While this may construe me as biased in the discussion, it is my passion and my experience that has rendered me so, and I hope to use this to alert others to the matter at hand so the course can be taken that best helps those that need it.

Because the narrative of unilaterally denying young transgender people puberty blockers is one of the most harmful pieces of public propaganda. While there will always be a balance to be maintained between helping those who need it and ensuring that it cannot be attained without due process, to have this discussion a full account of the facts must first be known. I will talk about the medical reasons and then go onto the effect this may have on a person's mental health.

During the transition, one will most likely be prescribed hormone replacement therapy. This affects much of the body's physiology, though some aspects are irreversible and the treatment must be taken throughout one's life. However, once a person has passed through puberty based on the gender they were assigned at birth, some of the changes made to their body during that process are defining and perhaps permanent.

For example, this could be facial hair, a broken voice or an Adam's Apple for a transgender female; or wider hips, breast growth, feminine facial bone structure or ovulation for a transgender male. Some of these can be mitigated with treatment or surgery, but some cannot. All, though, do lessen the ultimate impact of any hormone replacement therapy taken after this process has resolved. For many, myself included, this presents an insurmountable barrier to the full expression of one's internal identity because there are now parts of our bodies we either must fight to change or simply cannot, no matter how much we might want to.

This is why I must still undergo regular facial hair removal treatments even years after I began my hormone treatment, or why I rarely expose my arms and shoulders for fear they carry the masculinity birthed in my first puberty. It is why I cringe at the sound of my voice, even after years of practice, because I am trying to drag up a voice that dropped into the depths of my chest. And it is why when I compare myself to a cis-woman, I know there is an unattainable division, a self-loathing comparison between what they get from birth and what I desire but can never have.

For those undergoing hormone treatment before their assigned puberty has begun, however, blockers are used to prevent it from occurring. This then means that the replacement hormones can have a greater effect on the body, allowing that person to express themselves more fully as the gender as which they identify. This occurs not just in preventing certain processes from taking place, but before a certain age, a person's bone still has some inherent malleability. But after puberty, they lock in place and cannot be moved or morphed without severe and invasive procedures. Hormone treatment, if taken in time, can subtly guide the skeleton to conform more closely to its cis counterpart, decreasing the barrier and division described above.

While blockers hold off the assigned puberty, this is not permanent. It only allows time for the correct course to be ascertained and the greatest benefits achieved should the transition be chosen as the better path. Should a person decide not to undergo the transition, the blockers can be removed and the assigned puberty can go ahead as normal if only delayed by a few years.

By restricting or flatly denying people below the age of eighteen such gender-related treatment, they are forcibly subjected to the permanent effects of their assigned puberty. This is extremely harmful to their mental health and may require surgery later to rectify if it can be afforded – if it is even possible. In preventing them from making a reversible decision, they are forced to experience an irreversible consequence that will most likely scar their bodies in a way that cannot be undone and in the end perhaps cause more harm than good.

This restriction can take place either through policy decisions, public pressure, or simply the fact that by the time a person has gone through the NHS waiting list, it will be too late.

Now, regarding a person's mental health.

Suicide, ideation, and self-harm among transgender individuals are proportionally higher than in cis people of similar age groups and demographics. Transgender people face constant and obstructing levels of abuse, discrimination, and inequality. According to the Stonewall website, two in five have had a hate crime committed against them in the last year, two in five young transgender people have attempted suicide, and one in eight have been physically attacked by colleagues or customers at work. And people wonder why we are scared to walk down the street, go to work, or even leave by the front door.

From a Stonewall School Report in 2017, which looked at transgender individuals under the age of twenty-four, of the 3717 responses, 84% had self-harmed, 92% had the idea to commit suicide, and 45% had actually attempted it. There were also reports of forms of bullying and harassment transgender and LGBT+ individuals suffer at a young age, even today.

By denying a young transgender person the medical help they need because they are told they are too young to know themselves, made to think they are wrong for feeling the way they do, and forced to live in a body that is not theirs until it is too late to change it in the way they envision, will only cause these numbers to rise. It will also normalise among the public that children neither need nor deserve help and will thus only increase the kind of daily abuse highlighted in the above report.

But this is untrue.

No one knows you better than you.

The amount of self-assurance it takes to come out to yourself, let alone friends, family, and society at large cannot be understated. Each day is an interrogation and each step outside the front door is a declaration.

It took me over a thousand days to receive my hormone treatment and only after being vetted by my GP, a psychiatrist, and two medical experts at the gender identity clinic. They will provide the same stringent criteria, perhaps more so, to transgender individuals under the age of eighteen. These are the safeguards already in place to ensure that those who receive medical treatment are those for whom it will most benefit. And in the meantime, should not a child be heeded, their concerns addressed, and the time allowed for them to come to terms with their feelings? If the transition is for them, they can be allowed through with the best possible start, but if they decide it is not for them, they can resume their assigned life without any permanent harm. There are no losers here.

But the system as it is, the long wait times and general public reticence around blockers and children receiving any kind of treatment, can cause many to commit suicide. This may seem the only escape to living as someone they do not want to be for what can appear an interminable amount of time.

If you wish to help transgender children, supporting policies that properly fund and staff the system that currently exists will have the best results. Allowing access to education, especially in a school setting, can help normalise the idea of gender beyond the binary at a young age to then work its way through the other rungs of society as time goes on. Let the experts inform the decision-making process, rather than giving into fearmongering rhetoric that denies a child even the chance to choose their future.

Otherwise, parents will be taught to think their child is just going through a phase, unable to truly know themselves because they are too young. Bullies will have the excuse they need to abuse their transgender colleagues because they will have been indoctrinated to see them as different, unworthy of help, and misguided for trying to be themselves. And more young transgender people may consider, attempt and, sadly, commit suicide. They will see it as the only escape from a situation that has trapped them in a form they despise and cannot now be changed the way they desire. All due to a faulty system and a society wide dogmatic refusal to heed their earnest protests.

Every year, on the 20th of November, members of the LGBT+ community gather around the world in huddled nightly vigils. The Transgender Day of Remembrance commemorates those lost in the preceding year to abuse, assault, murder, mutilation, and suicide.

As we shiver, protecting our candles from cold winter wind, a list of names is read. Each one is a death that could have been prevented. Each one is a life unlived. Each one is potential unfulfilled.

Please do not let that list get any longer than it already is.

Summary Table of HRT Effects

Effect	Expected Onset	Expected Maximum
Fat Redistribution	three to six months	two to five years
Decreased Muscle Mass	three to six months	one to two years
Softening Skin	three to six months	Unknown
Decreased Libido	one to three months	one to two years
Decreased Erections	one to three months	three to six months
Breast Growth	three to six months	two to three years
Decreased Testicular Volume	three to six months	two to three years
Decreased Sperm Production	Variable	Variable
Slowed Body Hair Growth	six to twelve months	>three years
Stopping of Male Pattern Baldness	one to three months	one to two years

Chapter Fifteen

Soul

One evening, during my third year at university, I was supposed to be revising for my first batch of final exams. Instead, I was cowed by the pressure and fell to making a series of lists to pass the time, and to distract myself. I find comfort in order and organisation. My favourite books. My favourite bands. My favourite albums. And my favourite movies.

At the time, *Forrest Gump* occupied the top spot, as it had ever since I first saw it as a child. I relished the performances, the humanity of the characters, the heartfelt connections, and the subtle humour. But not long after, it was challenged by a newcomer. Richard Attenborough's *Gandhi*. It only took two viewings for it to snatch the lead and has remained there untouched ever since.

It is a film that has stuck with me and to which I turn once a year or so to humble myself and to try and understand what drove him. A man with a bamboo stick that brought down an empire. That film, those years ago, started me on a journey that even now I struggle to put into words. It has inspired every action, every story and attempted novel, and influenced most every thought since.

It has given me a perspective on my life. To life in general. And the transition. I needed such help. While perhaps the most vivid in terms of progress, it has been one of the toughest periods I have ever experienced.

Confusion, denial, loathing and realisation, interrogation, isolation, commiseration and celebration, examination, administration, discrimination and medication. Through it all, I have intended to live fully as me, as who I am and who I discover and forge for myself. But no matter how far I go, there always seems to be one more step to take.

It never wants to end.

The Internal Transition

True to its name, the transition is a period of immense change. While I have dealt so far with the general, the administrative and the emotional, and will later cover in depth the physical, I do want to address the transition of the soul, of the person underneath. This will be more personal, perhaps more abstract and not wholly applicable. You are free to ignore me, skip over this section and continue on as before. But I wanted to write it first for the sake of completion but also to fully capture the idea of growing into a new person. I want to demonstrate, as succinctly as I can, the manifestation of that 'as well as' I mentioned before.

But I am a stuttering, imperfect writer. Even now I struggle to find the phrases to give these thoughts meaning, yet I need those words now more than ever. I need their help. Gender dysphoria never lets you rest. It is constant. No matter where you are, who you are with, or what you are doing, it is there. Hearing a slip in your voice, a change in your stance or how you sit, seeing someone else presenting effortlessly as your desired gender and feeling the heartache of envy. It is a shadow that hangs over you, day and night, in dreams and in waking. It is a reminder that you are not right, that you are not what you should be. The transition is about stepping out from under that shadow and living as you are, have always been, and no longer hidden away.

In my case, this came from a theme that has permeated this journey since it started, a philosophy that has kept me going through all the indecision and convocations. It is the destination to be reached at the end of all of this – a way of living life in the sun. The theme I started to contemplate when I first watched *Gandhi*.

I could not believe there was someone so selfless and so committed to that idea of selflessness. He would raise others up and be content with that, weaving a loincloth alone in the sunset wilds as his country struggled with his message and the goal of independence. What struck me was just how far those he met, those his words reached, could grow because of what he inspired in them, and the culmination of their actions was traced back to this single, humble man.

In me, this line of thinking eventually formed around the idea of identity, that of self, place, and remembrance. I found it oddly fitting, seeing how much turmoil my identity had been going through in recent years.

From the start, I was battling against the notion of being what others wanted me to be. It was, I believe, the only way I knew how to not feel alone, to feel like I belonged to something bigger than myself. And that was my identity: one made for others. It did not matter what I was on the inside because no one got to see it. Not even me. I contributed nothing unique about myself, and thus, I did not really exist. I was forgotten as soon as you walked out the door. I forgot myself.

And that, I think, is what I have been trying to say all this time when I talk about how transitioning has given me control of my life. Not only has it given me a chance to take hold of the administrative side of things, but it has made me surer of what I am inside and given me the ability to construct and express that identity. I have the tools to be perceived and have that perception impact the world around me. I walk the delicate line between self-identity and selfishness, self-expression and conformity. But, for the moment at least, I walk sure.

I Sit Alone with the Moon

The stage has been my home for pretty much my entire life. No matter what theatre I am in, it feels familiar. I know its shape and curves, its nooks and crannies, its secrets and hidden crawlspaces.

It is ironic that it was only on a stage that I felt truly comfortable. While I was up there, with the lights on me, the audience waiting for the next line or note, that was the only time when I could stop being me. It was as if I could finally be recognised, and had the instructions to follow and the permission to do so. I knew what I needed to do. And I remember very little of what happened onstage, only when something went wrong or I broke character for a moment. The rest was something else. Someone else.

But while I could pretend, there are the rehearsals and workshops that surround any production, where the proximity to other people forces you to either interact or isolate yourself ever further. Without even realising it, I chose the latter. I did not go to the pub after workshops with the rest of the company. I read books in rehearsals during the gaps when I was not needed. I kept my headphones in and said nothing beyond what the script dictated because that was the only time people listened or cared that I existed.

But this could never last.

During one workshop we were split into pairs and tasked to tell each other a story from our past. We would then choose one and both recount it to the group, trying to present to them that it was actually from each of our own respective pasts, not the other's. Even though my partner and I went with one from my childhood, no one guessed. One of them said: "Who knows if it's L-'s. They're a mystery."

At this point, I had seen these people for two hours or more every week for nearly two years and they did not know a single thing about me. They could not even tell the truth from a convincing fiction. They did not care that I was there. If I stopped turning up, it would not have made a difference.

That was a wake-up call for me. I had to ask myself why this was the case and why I had allowed it to happen.

I began to realise this when I watched the Studio Ghibli movie, *When Marnie Was There*, for the third time.

Like every Ghibli feature, it is beautiful and mysterious, and you can tell a lot of thought, imagination and heart went into making it. There is something beneath the surface even if you cannot see it your first time through. I always felt like I connected with the protagonist, Anna: her loneliness and her search for acceptance in the company of Marnie. And I tried to figure out why. Why was she going through this journey? How did it relate to her past? How did she overcome it? It was on that third viewing that I realised, and the word glowed neon behind my eyes.

Neglect.

It hit me and I wept.

I cried because I understood for the first time what I had been doing. I will avoid saying more about the movie, in case you want to see it, but I will say that I could draw some parallels between Anna's situation and my own and how we both dealt with loneliness. I was always the outsider, in the school body, among my friends, and even among my family. I was alone for long periods, not helped by a rather tumultuous assigned puberty.

In school, I found that the only way I could get and maintain attention was by being exactly what people expected me to be. I fulfilled the image they had of me, that of the attentive, successful student they felt justified in hating. I did all I could to perpetuate that image, not only for my self-validation in terms of academic success, but because I did not want to upset what people thought of me.

I engaged only in superficial conversations. I never behaved wild or out of turn. I never said anything without considering it for so long that when I finally came to speak the moment had passed. It was not much, these stories others had of me, but I would do anything to keep my role in them going. Little though they might have been, they were the only company I had.

Even among my friends, I rarely opened up about myself. I maintained the traditions of social interactions. I kept to my niche and my presence was sometimes forgotten. I had my place and did not want to do anything to upset them lest I lose the group. Looking back, it does not make much sense, but it was such a foundational fear that it took me years to reconnect with my old friends after coming out as transgender. Even then, I found it difficult to upset the established script.

And during my teenage years, my family was going through some issues that, I was worried, would tear the whole thing apart. I will avoid details for their sake, but in that turmoil, I discovered that by being perfect, by succeeding in school, by always being on time, by never rocking the boat, I could provide a release, a respite from the storm and perhaps help hold things together a little while longer. I was the emotional rock upon which the rest of the family was built. At least, that was how I saw it. They relied on me and therefore I was not allowed to change, or do anything untoward, lest everything come crashing down around me.

I never wanted to hurt anyone. I did not want to risk the image they had. Why worry them? And I feared being more alone than I already was. If I opened myself up, would they still like me? If I showed just how sad I was, would they stick with me or abandon me because I was too much trouble? Or if I tried to be like them, if I forced myself to be loud and the centre of attention, would they like me or just think me a diva?

The result?

I did nothing.

From the ages of ten to twenty, this was my personal mantra without even knowing it. I was fine on the outside to maintain the only vassal I had. I fooled myself into thinking I was happy, that I had a place. But when I went to university and lost my old friendship group, lost my family, lost the old school bullies, I acted out the whole thing again with a different forced identity and saw then just how hollow I was.

I had filled the emptiness with books, writing, acting, music and studying. But not friendship. Not love.

No relationship had lasted more than three months, and I think that was because I had nothing to give beyond a surface detail. I had never learned to do so. On those rare moments when someone cared enough to scratch beneath and uncover all I had to give, I felt truly content, but it was fleeting. They would leave and I would go back to my old ways. The cycle continued. The only method I had to my madness.

I was so desperate for an identity, any identity, that I was willing to put on the one I was given. I believed in all kinds of delusions if it meant I could be accepted. I was validated by an external source. But should that source leave, I was faced only with the lack of any personal gain. I had done nothing with my time. I could be forgotten. For that decade of effort, there was no meaning for me being there. I could just fade into the corner and disappear.

Paradoxically, I do not regret this neglect. I missed out on a lot of years because of it, but it gave me skills that I use and rely on today. Beyond the talents I developed in playing guitar, acting and writing, the love I have for music and books, all I have striven to do to fill my void has made me a well-read, well-rounded individual with a wide toolset with which to communicate myself. It made me mentally strong because I had to weather many years of loneliness, pressure, and dependence. I made myself meet and exceed others' daily expectations to earn their respect and attention. It made me a perfectionist, someone ambitious and who always tries to do their best. I persevered through all kinds of storms to merely keep up the façade.

The transition has given me a chance to start over, to carry on those parts of me I like, that serve me well, and to re-evaluate those I find wanting. But even this was a challenge. I met my own emptiness, mourned the time I spent in its hollows, and forgave myself for the time I had wasted. Even now, I feel a tremendous sense of guilt for any day not used to its fullest. I came to terms with my loneliness and how little I inherently mattered. I contended with the unspeakable denial and anger that came with such loss after so much struggle. And I faced up against those expectations that had moulded me and upon which others, such as my family, relied. What before was the crutch upon which I was built was now a barrier to being all I could become. They did not want to lose the person they knew. It factored into the depths of their own identity. But change is the name of the game. To me, that is what it means to grow up.

It is why I have always hated the interview question: "Where do you see yourself in five years?"

Because the only true answer is: "I haven't got a clue." Five years ago, I was a far cry from the person I am now, and in five years I am going to be different again. The act of labelling only gives you something to lose. I am more interested in what I am going to find. The identity that I have made and continue to make. Not the one I was given.

Just Passing Through

Just after I first sought a referral, I travelled to Edinburgh to perform at the Fringe Festival. At this point, I had recently come to terms with the fact of my dysphoria and the solution I needed. Despite this, I was playing a male character in the show and, as I have mentioned before, decided to test myself by growing a beard. For three months, I intentionally trapped myself in the 'wrong' body. I hated it. That much should be obvious. But it was a useful and revealing experiment.

There is a significant self-interrogation involved in the transition, part of which is to test yourself against society. For those months, I played my part to perfection and hated myself for it. It seemed that I could only find identity in opposition. But I always felt guilty that in transitioning I was being selfish, focusing too much on myself and not considering enough the feelings of those around me. I feared I was robbing them of their idea of me, and in that thievery removed a part of their identity as mother, father, brother, or friend. Was this wrong of me? Would it not be better if things could go back to the way they were, to a simpler time where things were good and quiet?

I wished for it at times, that I didn't feel this way. Sometimes I still do. I might have been nothing when alone, but in the company at least there was the pretence of community.

Wandering the Royal Mile, seeing drag queens and guitarists, dancers and jugglers, actors and acrobats, I was alone and silent, hidden in a beard and thinking myself invisible. Was it good to never change, to have others be happy in their idea of you? Or was it evil, on both our parts, to hold ourselves back and never test the other, never allow us to be all we could be? In such struggles, we enable each other to grow, to find, to overcome, and to push forward when the next boundary rolls around.

But when I look back, I must ask what would I have become had I remained so constant. A lot has happened since that 2015 trip to Edinburgh, and while I still feel like I have missed out on so much, I have experienced more than I otherwise would have. Had I not transitioned, how many more years would I have wasted as an identity forged by others? Would I have run down the clock never having been anything more?

Two Roads Diverged in a Yellow Wood

The Robert Frost poem has two different interpretations, and while only one was intended by the author, they are both valid and lead to interesting conclusions.

The first reading I heard was from the film *The Dead Poet's Society*, where Robin Williams' teacher uses its final line, 'I took the road less travelled by and that has made all the difference' as an idiom to carve your own path in life, to strike out from the crowd and be something totally unique. The second is from the poet himself when he admitted that the poem had been written almost as a joke to a friend to express the redundancy of feeling regret for past decisions, the time wasted toiling over the choice and holding onto what could have been.

Due to the transition, I am a person with a keen affinity for regret. The years unfinished and the waiting forced upon me, unable to give myself fully to life, is part of that. But moreover, my mind traverses the 'What if?' territories more than perhaps is healthy. When I was younger, I did not know 'transgender' was a thing. I did not even know the word, let alone the concept itself, existed. For that reason, I had limited insight into why I felt so disconnected and alone, why I never felt comfortable in my own skin or how I fitted into my social groups.

But what if I had known? What if I had heard that word earlier? What if I had started experimenting sooner? What if I had been born female from the start? While these will forever remain unknown, I cannot help but wonder about them and the times and experiences I have missed because of them.

I did not live a great portion of my youth because I was so enclosed in an unwanted form without knowing what was wrong. I found it difficult to make new friends. I stood alone at parties. I rarely got drunk. I was fastidious to a fault. I planned everything to suit the image of the perfect child and student. I never had the wild moments that can so define and colour those years. And I hate that I was like this.

I feel like I have missed out on a lot, as if, knocking on thirty, I have barely even started. And while all the years I did live have cumulatively built to make me the person I am today, tending towards improvement, I cannot give up on those other roads in the wood, wonder what they might have held and if their product would have been happier than the one here today.

There is an infinite variety of them. Some last. Some do not. Some are wondrous. Some are not. I can't leave a part of the map unexplored. What do the shadowed corners of my island hide?

So, I understand what Frost was trying to say, to let go of this division. In refusing, how much more time have I wasted wishing to make good on those other roads? What do I deny myself because I am attempting to backtrack and go left instead of right? I do my best to follow Frost's advice and forget those alternate routes, but it is not easy to do. The amount of time I dedicated myself to a single path not knowing there was another all along is hard to simply take on the shoulder and keep moving. I hope that with my transition I can accomplish this, and create a future, but for the moment I am stuck in limbo between the two extremes: craving the comfort of the familiar, to not lose all I was and all I might have been had things gone differently, and desperate to escape everything I once was so as not to waste any more time.

This leads to the reading of the explorer going against the crowd. There is no original wisdom in saying that it can be exciting and rewarding to buck the trend to strike out somewhere new. It leads to new experiences, meeting new people, forming new bonds and memories, and perhaps earning recognition. It is time well spent to make life interesting, unexpected, and worth living. While this is true, it must be tempered with an element of caution, the risk well catalogued. However, that said, it is, to me, one of the most successful ways to fashion a completely unique identity.

Whatever is achieved, whatever is created, will be wholly your own. Whatever it feeds back to you creates an evergrowing, self-propelled person. But that does not mean it is easy. It takes courage and fortitude to go against the tide, to risk isolation through separation, not knowing what might be found along an undiscovered route. It is scary. Trust me, I know. To do so, you must relinquish something, an identity previously held, with its accomplishments and connections, its possible futures and self-made markers.

Whether that is a price worth paying is up to the individual. Frost thought it was. Myself? I want to believe it is, but as I said I find it hard to completely remove myself from the years that formed me. It may be that I am wrong to think in such a way, but I nonetheless despise myself when I slip back into old routines and old ways for the mere comfort, for the lack of knowing how to be anything else.

Yet they kept me safe, and informed me how to behave and interact. They gave me a way to be and a place to belong in those small circles that responded to my particular disposition. It might not have been the world, but it was better than nothing. It was my little corner. It was dark and familiar. It was all I had.

However, the transition demands something different. That method can no longer apply. My life and routines, the image I built, and the connections I fostered cannot survive. I played my hand and changed how I am perceived. The old ways will not work. I look to what is to come, a unique future wholly my own, but also fear tackling the unknown without my safety net, and I regret what alternatives I have been denied because of the lot I was given.

I sense time slipping. The days pass quickly. The years shorten. I am terrified of the end and want to fill what time I have with as much as I can, yet I cannot. There is no way I can. The years have been spent. What is done cannot be undone.

My only options are to try the best I can with the material I have to fashion something devoid of predisposition and open to all the possibilities that yet remain, or hunker in the cocoon for pleasure and warmth, following the plan to meet achievement and lonely company, and never face what I have missed.

It is a battle still very much being fought and will perhaps never be decided. I see the geography, the forces arrayed as they are, and understand the tactics and strategies on both sides, and yet the stalemate endures.

Maybe you will have better luck.

Stardust

Over the years, I have found a measure of harmony in the person I present to the world and the one I feel on the inside. It gives me power. Because we are not only formed by our internal progression, but by how we affect the world and how the world returns that favour. Our identity is a bizarre conglomeration of self-belief and external reaction, a marker of how far we have come and how far we are willing to go.

I think we have all felt that warm glow when witnessing pure goodness, a harmony at the pieces of life. Perhaps this has something to do with legacy. Good acts enable novelty, new experiences, thoughts, feelings, interactions and friendships. They help improve upon what was before and further impart their goodness onto others. It might only be a slight change, but it is one from which the world can continue to grow. A cycle, a feedback loop, a rippling outward, all growing stronger and surer as a result. Therefore, regardless of how small the initial act might be, it echoes, felt in ancestry far beyond its inception. The act survives and inspires, lasting for as long as its thread persists, as does the person who precipitated it. They might be nameless and unspoken, but they are never forgotten because the deed lives on in the blessed memory of its initial act.

And I think we have all wondered at the horrific pointlessness of evil acts, how they seek only to serve the perpetrator. Whatever the act is, be it large or small, it is a matter of isolationism. Cut off from the rest of the world, it is created either at the harm or disregard of others. This is what makes me sad. All that pain, all that hurt, only serves to hold back the current for a little while so the few that benefit can be comfortable, wealthy or powerful for a time. It perpetuates stagnation, and come to the end, we realise what potential might have otherwise been lived. 'Momentary masters of a fraction of a dot', as Carl Sagan would have said. There for a time, seemingly untouchable in the hurt they cause, and then gone and the pain eventually washed away. Nothing remains but the trauma and the wasted years. Soon, not even that, for all those lives, torment, and stolen chances.

The terms good and evil might be too much of a catch-all, each with their subtleties and crossovers, but as I have come to understand the further reaches of these definitions, I see them more as a guide to action.

That action might just be something as simple as helping out a friend, but they could now go onto new situations, bolstered by the confidence of that event, and carry the memory with them and act in a similar way with anyone else they meet. The act percolates and propagates and benefits life at every interaction in a small but lasting way. We exist then in this cumulative history, from which we are made and which we make in turn.

When I write now, or even when I read or watch films and TV series, I find myself breaking down what I am writing or what I am seeing to these two core concepts. It helps distil the truth behind the motives. I see both almost everywhere, even in my own history. Dressed in rationale, illusions or tales, and regardless of dogma, creed, background or constitution, these are the key motivators and progressors of growth and conflict. It is something I have tried to invest in my own life, to act as little as I can for my own needs or desires, but to use my time and energy to help others and give them the chance to laugh to fill the void.

Because if you refuse to change, sticking to tradition and routine, the days are then in service to maintain that routine and any greater agency is lost. Yet if you allow yourself to be changed, for your views, opinions, and actions to be altered by what you experience, then you can grow past those prior routines and discover something new and unexpected. You then have the chance to influence new aspects, and new people, try new things, and matter beyond where you were a short while before.

I used to be quiet and reserved, with the idea of being the good student and the good child, worried that if anyone got too close, I would scare them away because I was so uninteresting underneath. I was what they wanted and needed me to be. But when I came out as transgender, I had to come to terms with the fact that I could no longer support that image. I had to make a statement of myself. I had to change. I had to take the other road.

Without the shackles of expectation, I could interact with people in a different way, and I found that I was a different person from what I had previously thought. I was more extraverted and confident. I put this into the world, into my friends and family, and it fed back. They wanted to have me around because we had a good time together. This meant I then had the confidence and opportunity to try new things, go on trips to places I had never been, go to clubs I had not been to before, to just try little things and fill my days with novel and interesting experiences.

Some I like, some I do not. A film I watch might inspire a new way of thinking. A trip might inspire a new hobby I could take up. Or I might find the limit of what I find pleasurable and focus my energies elsewhere. Then something will happen and I will change again, and start down a brand new road of little things.

This is what I think it means to live in alignment. This is, to me at least, the true treasure of the transition.

Total self-identity to the exclusion of all else is a fallacy to give comfort in the face of ennui, an excuse not to change. But when you accept the fact that identity is, by its very nature, a transient thing, that the labels you stick upon your forehead change over the years, sometimes even over the course of a day, then you can let yourself be moulded by what you experience, and then you can grow and influence in response. It allows for unparalleled control, of making your life your own, as far-reaching as your imagination can conjure. It is a harmony of spirit and body that offers you a chance to exist outside the boundaries of atom and flesh.

Much of life, I have found, is coming to terms with the fact that one day it is going to end. Each second is a precious jewel that, once beheld, can never be reclaimed. Maybe the fervour of the endless self is a way to stall this realisation, to mistake time as static and our parts as forever relevant. A perfect person is frozen in a perfect moment. But this illusion shatters. Sooner or later, the crisis comes. For me, this has been much of the transition. Though I can reason and logic until my mind gives up, the fear is always there.

So, how do we make our life matter beyond our allotted time? How do we quell the fear of the reaper? I do not know the answer, but the idea to which I hold is one which I have spent this chapter poorly explaining: the hunt for harmony in identity. And that word is the key. Life is a search for identity, for a way to matter, a place to belong, to have our life, this speck of stardust in a universe beyond our imagining, means something.

If you hold to the self as this royal thing, as I did in my teens, not out of loyalty but out of habit, out of a lack of any way out, then you sacrifice your agency. Your reach ends at the limit of the self, a feedback loop where you create the world only to support your held identity. Meanwhile, the world moves on without you. Your bubble may last for a generation or two, held in a transient permanence, but then it is gone, in name, act and remembrance. It is all grown, evolved and changed despite your efforts.

But if you let your identity be a fluid thing, a congregation where you affect the world and allow it to grow, then that world will turn around and throw new things at you, forcing you to change in response. And you will provide new stimuli, and these will be returned, on and on. Forever. Each new branching pathway is made possible because of your input. As long as they persist, in whatever form, in whatever evolution, you will be a part of them. Your identity will have grown beyond the bounds of flesh to incorporate the whole of this amalgamation, and all others that together made it so.

This is why the greatest good you can do is to enable someone else to be a part of this journey, and the greatest evil is to deny them entry into the mad experiment that is life. This is why good always wins. Evil courses lead to this pocket of recurrent behaviour that exists only within its own bounds and to maintain its creators. But when they go and their influence wanes, the world moves on from the mess left behind, and we mourn those that were trapped by it.

We tend towards goodness due to the gratification we feel when we embark upon one of those new branching paths. Be it by our own will or to offer the chance to another, it will ripple outwards forever, building and morphing, but carrying forever within its structure our small influence and any influence we thus inspire. We become immortal within this ever building wave to the good. This is where we meet, to mould and matter within this great, amorphous collective endeavour.

I often think about the end of time, where every star dies and even the smallest atoms are ripped apart, and how our time will be measured at that moment. It is hard not to be drowned by the terror and meaninglessness of such a moment, the lack of any celestial report card to validate our efforts and tell us we did well to get as far as we did.

Instead, I look backwards, to every life and every year that got us there and find worth in the hope that every life, every year, was made, by our selfless efforts, a good life, a good year. That, for its time, humanity was happy. It did great things. It made every life worth living in what it could create and what it could carry forwards for others to continue.

We were a part of that. That was who we were. We were faced with the void, and we laughed.

This is our identity.

This is my identity.

This is what I have found through my transition and why I am happy to live now as I am, my internal identity presented without filter to the outside world. What I give to friends and strangers alike, in the smallest as well as the grandest gestures of conviction and care, are communicated beyond the confines of my body to live in what we together inspire, even if it be but a fraction of that end.

Evil and hatred are swallowed up, reviled, and eventually forgotten for the short-term harm they cause, the progress they stunt and the agency they deny. But goodness lasts forever. And in myself, I can be a force for good in this world, no matter how small.

As is perhaps typical of life's serendipity, I found the kernel of this expression in the unlikeliest of places.

I was updating my Steam software, the video game installation programme, and there was an option to run it on the usual gamut of operating systems, but also this offshoot of Linux called Ubuntu. Curious about this new word, I looked it up on Wikipedia and found that it is derived from a South African philosophy that literally means: 'Humanness'. Or, and this is what stuck with me: 'I am what I am because of what we all are'.

Perhaps this is the most succinct way I can summarise the ramblings of the last dozen or so pages. I have been given the chance to be shaped and in that, I have found myself. With that knowledge, I can help shape the world around me and give that same chance to others. I then become not only what I am, but all that I enable in those I meet and touch. I have never liked determinism for this very reason. You never know what you are going to find. So perhaps 'Influentialism' is the better term.

I wonder if this is what I felt when I first watched *Gandhi*. It may well have been, in part, the philosophy that inspired Gandhi himself when he was in South Africa, fighting against the racial injustices committed against the Indian population there. But instead of a bamboo stick and a loin cloth, I have a guitar, make-up, and high heels. I will never help topple empires, but I can change social norms.

I will not have a nation mourn my passing, but I have now the capacity to give the world a little bit of good for my being here.

Because I can now give myself to life. I can do that. I have that power. I need no longer live by the script, but through the alignment of my internal identity and external presentation, I can start to write my own. I can give those I love and those I have never met the chance to smile in a way all their own, just as I was given. I can be sure that whatever future comes from this, it is made up of those smiles, an endless rippling unto eternity. And I can be happy with that. I can be remembered for that. It may not be my name or any gaunt legacy, just the cumulative identity to which we can each add in our own little way, the far-reaching progress we inspire in lovers, in friends, and in strangers.

Part Two

A Little Hormonal
The Medical Transition

Chapter One

The Performer's Paradox

The following section of this book will document my journey through hormone replacement therapy (HRT). I will be discussing in detail the anatomical and emotional changes I experienced, for reasons I have already outlined. The content for this came from individual entries I wrote for myself during this period that mostly coincide with the testosterone-blocking injections I have every three months.

That interval allowed for enough information to see a trend and note the differences between each, but not so much that they blended together to form an indistinct, extended present. But as these recollections were captured more in the moment than much of what has come so far in this account, which has been augmented heavily by a lens of hindsight and experience, it may carry a distinct tone and focus.

It will not have the same omnipresent perspective. These are my accounts while in the midst of a personal seismic shift, viewed from the ground to highlight with as much clarity as I can the results of HRT. And much of what I felt then I still feel now, and I will use tense to mark this in the text. I want this whole section to hopefully dispel any misinformation already out there, provide transparency for those external to the process, and alert those on their own transition to what may lie ahead so they need no longer fear the unknown.

And so, three months after starting my treatment, I began. It seemed as good a place as any. I knew it would take months to years for any changes to become noticeable, let alone defining, but to capture the entire transition I needed to work from a baseline. Only then could I see how far I had come and realise the many additions that accumulated to create the person I aimed to be.

Because, during my transition at least, I could not find a comprehensive account of what it was like being on hormones. Going in, such an unknown terrified me. There was no knowing what would change besides the general list of side effects given to me by my doctor or found on the Wikipedia page. Even what I gave above in the hormones chapter is based upon such information. They present generalities, a high-level view, capturing and condensing the tales of thousands over the course of years. But they fail to illustrate what it is like to live every day with this treatment. So, I wanted to give my thoughts and recount the effects, both emotional and physical.

When I started, I felt comfortable and almost validated in my presentation. It caused me to think about the nature of this change. It sparked a conflict in me.

As I have said, I was always a quiet child, mature for my age, more of an observer, and emotionally resilient but otherwise disengaged. This was out of necessity but became a place of familiarity and security. To keep myself occupied, I learned valuable life skills: independence, discipline, fortitude and organisation. I took up music, writing, video and card games, read every book on the shelf, and then built a new shelf with my dad on which to put more books.

I do not regret any of them. However, I do regret the loneliness this caused my teenage self and the loneliness that continues, in part, to infect my life today. It has diminished, for reasons I will come to, but that insular place nonetheless exists in the corners of my heart. It is a retreat where I know the rules and where I can make progress on the things I find enjoyable. But I do so alone.

The conflict comes because being transgender makes that retreat harder to reach. By the very fact of my existence, I am on display twenty-four hours a day. Every walk down the street draws looks, comments, hoots, honks and wolf-whistles. There is nowhere safe outside my front door. I am under surveillance and possible threat either by people who would misconstrue my lifestyle and treat me as something I am not, or simply perceive me as wrong or lesser for being a woman.

Violence against transgender people is a reality of the day, as are sexual advances, attempted pick-ups and propositions. This is perhaps the furthest I could get from who I used to be and the role I used to occupy. And yet, in some way, it is no bad thing. Overcoming and enduring these have made me more confident, more outgoing, and more willing to put myself out there and try new things. Those years and skills that led me here inform a strange, unique mixture. But there is still a difference, a player of two parts yearning for both exits.

When under such scrutiny, part of me seeks the comfort of the old role, to stay inside and write, sing, play the guitar, and finish the latest video game. This I know. Here, I do not need to put anything on to be accepted. And yet, another part takes the calls and hoots and admiring looks and wants desperately to be the one they see, the full-blooded cis-female able to exist without qualm or reservation. I want to drop on the dance floor or flaunt it on a summer's day. Either way, I end up confused and scared. With the former, I lose the steps taken to get me here. And with the latter, I am once again acting to expectations, to the social standard of the gender I aspire to be. Either way, I betray my core. Either way, I lose.

Now that I was starting hormones, it was impossible not to feel some doubt, a questioning of what led me to this precipice. I was forced to ask why I came out as transgender. Why did my life lead me here, and why has it manifested as a question of gender? I know and have tracked the acts through cause and conclusion. The path of logical steps leads from one to the next, but why to this state, this antipode of the conscientious student? I used to answer all the teacher's questions and was a friend but to a select, trusted few. I kept my head down, slid under glances and played the part for the solace it gave me. Why has gender taken me so far to the crux of a forking river?

I do not know.

I honestly have no idea. I have been told that I am smart for seeking the comfort of the familiar, for only speaking to those friends with whom I have something in common, but on how much am I missing out? What could I be experiencing in its stead? Something new? Something great? Or something that would lead me down a different, unexpected road?

And the biggest question I am forced to face is why gender? Why this upheaval? Is it because by being transgender I must be visible, tested and adaptable? In that case, is all this a performance, an experiment to convince people, myself included, that I am no longer that person? Is this all just an escape from some partially undesired identity? Or is it a true change, a bizarre mixture of new and old? I believe it is the latter and feel that in the everyday, but the question lingers.

There also comes another matter. When alcohol loosens a stranger's tongue and lowers the social barriers, I suddenly become the herald of the community, forced to raise awareness, explain and almost justify myself. Some people may want to be that, a champion for a community with such low visibility, but I at first did not want to be one of them.

I did not want to be the token that people go to with their queries about gender. I did not want to have to come out in every new conversation. I just wanted to live my life and be happy with who I am. How can I do that with this perhaps implied expectation to be a voice from the rooftops? Because then, I would stop being a woman having a good time and become instead another transgender person having the same discussion for the hundredth time with the hundredth stranger while being probed, judged and interrogated.

And I feel bad for admitting this.

Just a day. That was all that I wanted. Just one day without the pressure to present and feel that I am hiding something or putting something on to do so. Will I ever escape the truth that I am transgender? Will it forever mark me out as different? Will I always be reminded in limitations, looks, glances and secret remarks that I am not quite what I want to be?

And is that even a bad thing?

It should not be, but then why does it still make me cry?

Just one day.

So, to keep me going, I take my hormones. When I do, these trials diminish. Because, more often than not, the happiest part of my day is when I finish lunch, pop that little blue pill from its foil packet and swig it down with a glass of water. I know it is building towards something – or at least I hope it is, a point where I can find the balance hidden here somewhere and move beyond these haunts. Perhaps I can even prove them wrong. For anyone struggling through something similar, hold onto these moments, these rare, pleasant hours. They lead somewhere better, I know it. I have glimpsed it. I have almost had my own one day. Even if I have not found it just yet.

Chapter Two

Three-Month Review

Continuing on from the last chapter, which spoke more about my mental state at the time of starting my treatment and how many of my doubts and resolutions have lasted to the present, this chapter is going to focus on the initial physical changes that occurred within the first three months. This section will be a road map of sorts, leading you through what you may be likely to encounter, alleviating any fears and highlighting stage posts along the way.

To begin we start with my general body shape. One of the major side effects of the treatment is that the body varies where and how it stores fat, typically diverting away from the stomach and depositing it in the thighs and hips. Much also goes to the chest to form the breasts. Upon starting my treatment, I took some basic measurements to gain an initial outline of my body. For this, I focused on my hip and chest circumference, as well as my waist to see how my weight would vary, and the thigh to see if any clots were forming. This latter part was recommended to me by my consultant when they were talking through the effects of HRT, oestrogen being a coagulant. If there is any tenderness or swelling, this might indicate a clot, and medical intervention will be required immediately.

I made a spreadsheet so I could track these changes through a series of basic graphs. I took measurements at three-month intervals to coincide with my injections, which quickly became chapter markers in the transition, points of similarity against which backdrop I could mark and measure the changes. While I only kept this spreadsheet going for the first year or so, it did offer a useful visual representation of how my body was adapting to the treatment and the trend you are likely to experience yourselves.

From what I saw in those opening months, there was little overall difference in the proportions of my body, at least not enough to be seen under the motion of clothes and in the stance of routine. However, through my measurements, while my waist and thighs showed little change, my hips did show a small broadening, their circumference increasing by a few inches. While it was only yet visible in the numbers, it was nice to know the treatment was working.

My chest followed a similar trend but to a far smaller degree. Breast formation, though, is one of the slower, longer-term side effects, taking several years to reach their maximum. Yet even in those first three months, I could feel fat deposits starting to develop in that area and a noticeable bump starting to form. They were almost like proto-breasts, for lack of a better way to describe them. They were too small to be seen through any clothing and my breast forms did not impede them, so I could continue to wear these without issue, as with my hips, it gave me hope that my body was responding in the way it was supposed to.

Alongside these deposits in the breasts, I did notice that my nipples became more sensitive than they were before. There was not much cause for this to play a part in my everyday life or any sexual activities, but it was still something I was aware of so it is worth noting that something similar may happen to you at this point in the treatment. You may find you like it, or if you do not you can make a conscious note to leave them be. The area around the breasts themselves also became increasingly tender, noticeable when I knocked or bumped them. This feeling would increase over the course of that first year.

My skin became softer over this period. While this was not as evident on my face, it was over the rest of my body, especially the lower back, chest, waist, arms and legs. This has continued and remains to this day.

There are different kinds of hair over the body, with leg hair being denser and more coarse than the hair on the small of the back, and with pubic hair being even more so again. While this latter group showed little change, the rest became softer and in some places even slowed or completely stopped growing. Perhaps aided by several waxing sessions, my leg hair now took over a week to become noticeable stubble and a further few days before a shave was required. Even then, there were patches and the hair was softer than I recalled from before the treatment.

The wisps of fair hair located around much of the waist, stomach and back became increasingly soft and barely visible under normal conditions. On the chest, I used to have a few flecks of hair, always having been relatively smooth here even before the transition. These disappeared completely. Frustratingly, however, the hair around my nipples has clung on obstinately and I must shave these every few days, even now. In the future, I may explore the option of hair removal in this area, but as it is hidden most of the time and more easily manageable, I will focus on other areas first.

Similarly, what hair was left on my face at this time after my first bouts of hair removal did not respond to the treatment to nearly the same degree. The few strands left, especially around the lips and chin, kept up the fight. I continued with laser hair removal during this time, but I found that they had reached the limit of what they could achieve. I soon stopped it to focus more on presenting day-to-day without the distressing need to grow it out and present as male for the session.

Moving away from the physical, the most drastic changes were both in my mood and in the more private areas. With my mood, in short order, I became a lot more emotional, susceptible to extreme swings from mania to depression, hyperactivity to despondency, depending on the situation and stimulus. The hormones acted like a magnifying glass for any emotion I might have been feeling at the time, and sometimes I found myself getting upset or angry without any discernible cause.

This aspect was especially distressing if intriguing in a morbid sense. I had always been able to keep a handle on my emotions and track the logic from cause to effect that did result in any reaction or outburst. Now, though, I was no longer in control to the same extent. I was being buffeted by the storm of my emotions, victim to its swells and droughts, and this would only become starker as the months went on.

For example, it was around this time that I encountered the problem with a new job I described in the chapter on the corporate world. This was where they would not accept my gender in their HR system and its connection to HMRC as I had not yet updated my passport. To make the adjustment, they would need a Gender Recognition Certificate or an updated passport, neither of which I could get at that time and especially not on such short notice. Where before I believe I would have been able to work my way through it with more candidness and forthright action, this instead threw me into a week-long spiral of depression, anxiety, hatred and self-doubt.

While I emerged from the other side with a game plan, which I put into motion over the following years and avoided the same issue again, it was frightening to not be in control of my own moods for the first time in my life. Even now, years into the treatment, I cannot always pinpoint the reason why I am feeling a certain way and must simply ride it out as best I can.

The strongest lesson I have learned through all of this, having come from the world of assumed male stoicism, is to let your emotions out. Allow them to be felt. It may be scary, but they are there for a reason, even if we do not always know why. I always kept my feelings bottled up for fear of disturbing the image I presented to the world and the company I was offered in what people thought me to be, but as these emotions fester they can become exponentially more destructive over time. But catharsis is a welcome balm. It gets the feelings out and lets them run their course, so you can continue with life on the other side, unburdened by their infectious, insidious, ever-rising tide.

My libido suffered the most drastic change in those initial months. My sex drive shut down completely almost immediately after my first injection. It was a startling difference. Before the transition but after I had come out as part of the LGBT+ community, I used to be a sexually active person, enjoying a frequent and healthy sex life. But since that first testosterone-suppressing injection at the start of the treatment, my libido simply vanished.

To this effect, my more personal sexual pastimes also utterly ceased, feeling unnecessary and with little to no response or satisfaction. One of the more bizarre consequences of the treatment was that my testicles shrank significantly, almost disconcertingly. Though there was no discomfort and, if anything, only made it easier to tuck for presentation purposes.

The reason for this sudden shift is in how the injection interacts with the body. The suppressant works over a two-week period, overstimulating the pituitary gland until it switches off. At first, this may cause an increase in the libido, but after it, in a single swoop, almost totally disables the body's ability to generate testosterone. On the other hand, the daily tablets, which build up oestrogen levels, work over the course of months to years.

Though I have not consulted with a doctor on this, I believe this creates a lay over period where there are low levels of all sexually stimulating hormones in your system, so the body has none of the chemicals it needs to power the whole process.

At the time I did not know whether this was temporary or permanent, but over the years, as the levels of oestrogen in my body increased to reach the required amount, my libido did return, yet to a drastically lower degree. Perhaps getting older has also had its own effect, but while I can have and enjoy sex now, it is not nearly as intense or frequent as before. Yet it is difficult to miss something that my mind and body no longer desire in the same way, and I am happy at the more settled level I have reached in time.

These are all the changes I had in the first three months since starting the hormone treatment. There will be more, and some continue to this day, with the one-year mark being of particular interest. I hope this has been informative and continues to be so. And for those who may be starting their own hormone journey, I wish you the best of luck. May the changes be rapid and pleasant.

Chapter Three

Emotional Instability

Expanding on the discussion about my emotional state from the previous chapter, this was perhaps the most noticeable effect of my treatment and the one that interfered most with my daily life. It even threatened my ability to work and, had it become any worse, could have cost me my job.

I want to raise this in its own section in more detail to normalise the psychological side of the transition, and HRT in particular, so you need not fear or be surprised if you notice yourself, or someone you love, behaving out of the ordinary after they begin their treatment. It is normal, and with time and help does become easier to manage, but it hit me harder than I thought it would. Aided by the physicist in me, I have always been a rational thinker, able to break down situations to their base components and figure out a way through. Yet this became more difficult due to the hormone treatment.

This job was new, and the one with which I encountered the issues with HR I spoke about in the preceding chapter and in the chapter on my life in employment. For the first time, I moved away from a job that allowed me to work from home and had to instead contend with commuting to and working within an office environment.

I have already explained why this is terrifying in its own right and only adds to the stresses of the job itself. And being a full-time role with a commute that could last at best an hour and a half, I completely lost any vocational outlet to help me cope with this change. I stopped writing. I could no longer focus enough to edit. I was almost too tired to play video games or watch movies. I simply did not have the time, energy or inclination. I would wake, work, eat, sleep and repeat. My day became a very dull *Edge of Tomorrow*, but one that caused me my own source of trauma.

Hormones magnified every emotion into the most extreme version of itself. They would build up throughout the day and bubble beneath the surface, always seeking a way out. I turned up to work almost in tears; when I got home, in a tired rage, I broke a set of headphones and ripped apart a shirt whose buttons would not cooperate; I sat despairingly at the train window, wondering if I should turn around and screw the consequences. I wept on the phone with my parents trying to find any strength to keep myself going. And when I forced myself through, every conversation was tainted with that tingling in your throat when you are about to cry. I was always on the edge, barely keeping it down.

But, on the flip side, when I was happy, I was ecstatic. My mind would run at a hundred miles an hour in the office or when I got onto a topic I enjoyed discussing. I became animated and engaged, everything else forgotten. I sang aloud walking down the street, even danced a little should the right song come on and if I was relatively alone. I smiled at passers-by, interacted with familiar faces on the commute, and broke the British etiquette of staunchly ignoring each other on the train. I never used to do this before.

Yet it only took one look, one odd eye, one leering van man or motorist's catcall and I was once more locked in my clammy meat-cage. The world became my audience and my judge. I powered through, for the job, for the life I was told I should have, but rationale deserted me more often than I liked. I sank ever further into myself, less considerate of those around me and saw myself turning into a person I did not like being. It was almost as though I was looking from the outside-in, witnessing this change and despairing at it but wholly unable to do anything about it. I was lost to the currents of the storm, helpless about where it would take me.

This was a new state of mind for me, being so ruled by my emotions. I am certain part of this, a large part, was due to the job and the change it introduced into my life. Well, it certainly did not help! It cost me more than I imagined – physically, mentally, and creatively – to pursue. I was emptied and without identity for my efforts.

But part of the blame rests with those little blue tablets.

I do not hate them for it, but I was unprepared for the significance of their impact. They do nothing on their own, but good becomes great and bad becomes devastating. I was unsure of how long this would last. Was it a symptom of the hormonal lay over period between the lost testosterone and slowly building oestrogen? Or is this only the first stage of what could become a permanent fixture of the coming years, instability tracking with the chemicals in my blood? I simply did not know, and that was equally as terrifying.

I sincerely hoped it was the former. There has always existed this implicit trust between the two halves of my brain, between the creative and the rational. Even when they were at odds there was a common language with which they could communicate, a level of understanding that allowed them to operate by the same set of rules. They each knew where the other stood and how to factor that into their thinking. But now this trust had been shaken. There existed a dichotomy, a mental split between the two, a balance on which I had relied my whole life without even knowing it was there. There had been a link between feeling and explanation, but now it was one or the other. I did not get to choose, and I never knew when they were going to switch or how far they would take me.

It was frightening, depressing, and foreboding.

But I tried my best not to take it all badly. Earlier that year, I was questioning what I wanted to do with my life. From the age of sixteen, I had been writing novels and I had reached the point where I did not know if I wanted to continue this hobby, beaten back as I had been by one slew of literary agents after another. Experiencing such uncontrolled and uncontrollable emotional wildness, however, reminded me just how important that facet was. It was how I cultivated and maintained that balance, how I exercised a routine and exorcised a near-religious catharsis. It was one so successful that I had never realised just how much solemnity and listlessness it had purged from me over the years, how much uncertainty I had moulded into directed thought. It gave me purpose, carved meaning from chaos and offered an ultimate aim to the day. Knowing that I had an even greater conviction to return to it, to recapture what, at first, hormones had stolen from me.

And screw the consequences.

I promise that there is a point to all this rambling. Anyone about to embark on hormones, already going through it or supporting someone who is – hold onto what you love over what you are 'supposed' to have. Your hobbies and your passions, whatever they are, will become your rock, your anchor, the centre-point around which chaos orbits.

And if it becomes too much, do not be afraid to re-evaluate your life to make it work best for you. Do not lean on tradition, routine or expectation just because they are what you have always done. Get out early. Get out often. Your happiness need not be dependent upon another's success or validation. Do not let time pass you by while you try to play a game whose rules no longer suit you, or perhaps have never suited you. Doing what makes you happy is what will give you the strength to see through the harder days hormones bring.

And they will be hard.

There is a delicate balance to each person, a tightrope that must be walked, and hormones are the dumbbells the madman makes you hold. Your passion is the net that catches you when you fall, the one thing you can trust at such a time. Use it, and never give it up.

Chapter Four

A Strange Kind of Settlement

I have always had, and continue to have, a mixed and complicated relationship with heckles and catcalls. On the one hand, their objectification and intrusion can be unwanted, the feeling of unfriendly eyes. But other times, the coarse validation of my femininity is something that can, depending on my mood, land with a grin. Because I am seen as the gender I have chosen. It is damning that this is how our society has it in mind to show its confirmation, but if that is all I am allowed, then I will take it.

My second job was one that required a lengthy commute and a lot more time out in the world, far more than I had been used to having up until that point. Having worked at home for over a year and a half, and the rest of my external exposure being in carefully curated social occasions or experimental shopping trips for which I had time to prepare both physically and mentally, to be thrust into situations and a routine beyond my control was startling and scary. I was also needed in the office and had to walk to the local Tesco's every day to get my lunch. I was therefore prepared for the trickle of catcalls and horns to increase at a proportionate rate.

This, however, I underestimated.

In the first fortnight, I was on the receiving end of half a dozen 'compliments'. And those were just the ones I noticed. Being the kind of person who never goes anywhere without the cocoon of a headphone concert to keep me company and protected, there could have been many more that occurred outside my periphery without me realising it. And I do not have eyes in the back of my head. I could never tell how people would treat me once they walked past. Would they turn and gawk at my body, or swivel and sneer at my retreating form?

What surprised me, though, was when they would launch their assaults. Most were on the walk home from the station, which was itself a monstrous trek over a steep incline, unsheltered from the sea's high winds. After a full day's work and struggling uphill through a British winter, I certainly looked far from my best.

It made me wonder whether they were commenting on my raggedness or on some measure of feminine grace I managed to maintain. Did they disparage my foolhardy attempt to present as my desired gender, or were the flecks to which I held enough to inspire their lustful, patriarchal appreciation? Their words were indistinct if clearly directed at me. Lost behind music, traffic and rising gales, their attention was well-aimed. But while the intent was hidden, it nonetheless concocted the same hoard of questions.

But this is not the only way by which I felt differentiated by the transition. Due to my increased time outside during peak hours, having to cross roads and scamper across traffic lights, I noticed people stopping a lot more to allow me to pass. This did not happen before I began the transition, but now, it is almost guaranteed a driver will stop with a smile and wave to let me cross. Whether this is something people do for women out of some sense of chivalry or to have more time to look, I cannot be sure, but it has made itself known in recent times. This, coupled with three particular moments I experienced in those early weeks of that second job, had a deeper impact than each individually should have had alone.

The first was at work. I was on a call to a fellow worker and the connection was patchy so I borrowed the mobile phone of someone else on the call. Because of this, I could hear myself every now and again received through the phone's speakers, picked up, perhaps, by the feedback loop of two microphones so close together.

I normally hate my voice, as most people do when they hear it out in the world. It has always been one of my greatest insecurities. Having come from being a noticeable bass back before the transition, it has been hard to keep away from such a sternum-shaking instinct. I fear that upon a word I will be called out as transgender because they can hear the ancestry in my voice. Indeed, the lone time my gender was questioned was because of my voice. But here, this time, I did not hate what I heard. It was not pleasant, by any means, but it was tolerable. That, in itself, was a victory.

Aside from a few people in HR, with whom I did not need to interact after my induction, no one at my new work knew I was transgender. Despite this, I was on my guard, ready to defend myself should the probes and questions come my way. But for my entire time there, no one raised an odd look, subtly targeted question or outright interrogation. For both better and worse, I was treated, as I suspect, a normal woman would. Having tested myself in such an outward-facing and challenging environment compared to what I had known, this all made me more confident in my appearance, the image I was presenting and the identity I was starting to inhabit.

The second moment should not have been anything significant, but it was almost a confirmation of a change I had been wanting since the start. It was the first time I had evidence it was visible. Wide hips were not something with which I was blessed from birth. My shoulders got there first. But during the early months of the hormone treatment, I did start to notice a greater curve, caused by those little tablets siphoning my slightly increased weight to my hips. This was something I always wanted, a key piece in the diorama of my ideal female form.

And it finally happened that someone independent noticed and appreciated them – in their own way, that is.

I was out walking and a man on a bike cycled past. He made no effort to hide his intrigue around my figure, eyes firmly locked on my midriff and hips as he arched about me at the turning. I did my best not to make like I had seen and to just keep walking, but I clocked his expression and the effect it had on me. I knew I should not reward or even want to desire such open objectification but to have someone admire a physical aspect for which I had been clamouring from the start was another victory for me.

It might have been superficial, and it probably was, but this was one of those moments that let me know that the world saw me as the woman I had spent years wanting and trying to be. The image I had of myself and the one I put forward were more aligned. I was no longer the victim of parcelling and perception, be it intentional or otherwise. It was a vote of confidence in what I was trying to achieve.

The last moment came later that same night. I was on my way back from a friend's house. It was on the other side of the city so I called myself a taxi. I was not then, and to a degree still, now, one to chat with a driver, partly due to the stereotypically assumed British social status quo but also because of my vocal dysphoria. Yet this one was more talkative than most.

Usually, I kept my sentences short and interactions brief for the same reasons above. I feared each word could be used against me, to out me, to render all my work moot by someone crowning past over the present. But there, on that night, we had a more in depth discussion than what I was used to having. Seeing his face in the rear-view mirror, I elicited from him no question, no query, no inquisitive look. I was just another fare chatting away the night.

With LGBT+ visibility at an all-time high, and awareness and education more easily accessible, I cannot be sure whether the people I meet on a daily basis are at all aware I am transgender. Perhaps they see it in an instant and take it in their stride, polite and respectful to a fault. Or maybe they honestly have no idea and treat me no differently as they would the cis person they perhaps expect me to be. I am inclined to believe the latter. Even with LGBT+ rights on the rise, we are still a drastic minority, the transgender community especially.

With such limited representation, how can I expect every taxi driver, cashier and office worker to be clued into the language, to know the behaviour upon which members of the LGBT+ community rely to not feel ostracised or vulnerable? These are delicate missives, definitions spinning upon the tips of subtle connotations, and acceptance felt in the mire of interpretation. Some of these, in my time and despite my best efforts, I have failed myself. The result is that I must not believe them prepared. The three scenarios above were organic, made in the moment with no planning, expectation or interaction beyond the usual social conventions, and yet I was accepted in these small ways. I did not feel afraid or uncertain. I did not need my silence and safeguards for protection or to escape examination.

All this caused a greater sense of settlement in my identity. Though it came at the hands of an insidious underside to our society, it nonetheless made me feel less like a special case and more like a normal person. It is hard to adequately describe, but anyone who has been or is currently on the transitional path, you will know how blessed this feeling can be. It was no longer just a group of friends or an understanding family, but the person on the other end of the phone, the passer-by, the cashier behind the counter, the colleague in the office. It was the world. And I was finally starting to feel like I was a part of it.

Need we ask for anything more than that?

Chapter Five

Six-Month Review

A lot was happening at this time of my life and therefore when I recount this particular milestone, it might be considered a bit of a mess. But seemingly in a flash, I was six months into my hormone treatment, trying to summarise all the changes that had been happening.

It was at this time that I finally got my passport updated and renewed with my new name, gender, and picture. Building on the outline I wrote about earlier in the chapter on changing my name, rather than doing it over the post or online, I opted to complete the process in person. I was heading to London anyway for a GIC appointment and thought it would be easier and quicker to speak to a person over the counter, rather than trade e-mails and phone calls back and forth.

The downside to this was that it did cost a lot more money, around £150 at that time to book the appointment slot. Though that did cover the passport itself as well. And I could explain the situation to the person behind the desk and get it all sorted right then and there.

Once I had my appointment time booked, I took my old passport and a completed application form from the local post office, with the countersigned section complete. I also prepared some photos in advance, which were also countersigned, and brought them alongside my deed poll, evidence of my new name in use – such as a utility bill or bank statement – and the letter from the GIC proving that I was transitioning for the long term.

Speaking through everything with the person behind the counter was easier than I expected. They barely batted an eye at the fact I was transgender and operated as though this was just another case to action as part of their day. They were understanding, and the only hold-up was that the photos I had taken with me were too bright for their scanners and I needed to redo them while at the passport office. Once it was done, everything was posted to me within a few days and that milestone was then behind me.

The only area that I wish could have gone better was the photo, but then very few people are ever happy with their passport image. It is not designed to be flattering. I had originally decided to get it done before going to the passport office. I was self-conscious about using the self-service booths for the awkward experience of seeing a giant rendition of my own face pop up on the screen to stare back at me. I was becoming more comfortable in my appearance, but certainly not that comfortable. Instead, there was a camera store nearby that took passport photographs, so I chose to get it done there. Sadly, though, their photos did not work out, as I mentioned above with the office's scanners and I had to go through it all anyway.

Still, it is an interesting path to investigate if you too are wary about the booth.

But I made it and I had my passport. I was official.

After that trip to the passport office, I was then onto the GIC to start my journey to surgery and speech therapy. For the former, all was on track regarding my hormone treatment, based on my blood test results, so I was asked to pick my surgeon and hospital preference.

This is the point that begins the lengthy trail to receiving gender reassignment surgery. I would only be added to the waiting list, however, once I had been on my hormones for one year and living as my gender for two, both of which were due to occur in spring 2019, this appointment taking place in November 2018.

There are also several preliminary consultations, where the surgeon examines your anatomy to determine the best course of action and whether any hair removal is necessary prior to the operation. As for breast augmentation surgery, they recommended only getting this after two years of hormone treatment.

As you cannot have two surgeries within close proximity to each other due to the recovery time of each and the stress it puts on the body, if you are looking to receive both sets of surgeries, my recommendation would be to liaise regularly with the NHS to determine their approximate timeline. Breast augmentation surgery must be done privately so has more freedom in when it can be arranged, so you can slot it in before or wait until after, depending on how everything lines up in your case.

As the waiting list is only ever getting longer for all consultations and appointments, let alone the surgery itself, it may help fill the time to receive breast augmentation surgery in this gap, if it is something you wish to have. You may find that after being on hormones for a number of years you come to like what you have grown and have no need for any enhancement.

For the main gender reassignment surgery, I was told at this appointment there would be a week in the hospital, followed by a month off work, three months of tenderness, and then many more of training and general recovery. I will cover this in more detail in the third section of this book, which tracks my eventually unsuccessful path towards surgery.

We then moved to the topic of speech therapy. I had opted at the start of the transition to go on the waiting list, just in case I ever needed it in the future. Thankfully, with my background in the theatre, I made good progress on my own using the techniques I had picked up over the years. I felt that I had reached a point where my voice could be used in conversation without it prompting someone to question my gender.

I did eventually have an appointment with the speech expert in a one-on-one consultation, and they agreed on the extent of my progress. My voice had come to rest naturally higher in my throat, with a softer intonation gathered over months of practice, and this had all come together as outlined in the earlier chapter on the voice.

However, at that point in the transition, I did still struggle when it came to projecting my voice and public speaking. I also found it hard to maintain my voice for long periods of time. I was still a member of several of my university society groups at this time, and in one of them, I was directing a show. While I tried to corral a noisy and unruly cast, I did hear my voice falling to a more familiar register for such activity. One of the producers said to me that they had not realised I was transgender until one of these moments. I knew then that more work needed to be done, so I decided to join the GIC's speech therapy group.

It ran its sessions once a month for a period of five months and focused on public speaking, projection and phone calls. These sessions were due to start in spring 2019, but while I was with the individual speech therapist, they gave me a good exercise to help open up my throat if I felt it tightening.

You rub your tongue across your teeth, top and bottom, clockwise eight times, then anticlockwise eight times. Then clockwise for six and anticlockwise for six. Then four, then two and then once, rotating both ways each time. This works the muscles in the throat, which hurts at first, but does help relax and open up the throat so that speaking becomes a lot easier.

And after six months of the hormone treatment, it was again time to quantify the changes that had happened to my body. Though I did encounter one obstacle I had not expected.

When my GP first prescribed my hormones, upon recommendation from the clinic, they had not done so on a repeat prescription. If you have the NHS app, you can check the status of your prescriptions and easily reorder them through there, but if they only issue them one at a time, speak to your GP surgery and hound them until they get it put on repeat for you. Much of the hormone treatment will last the rest of your life and it will make everyone's job far easier if it can be on repeat for you.

I had to go to the GP in person every few weeks to pester them about getting a prescription for my tablets or upcoming injection. There was no trick to this beyond persistence and doing my best to annoy the receptionists. This is the greatest piece of advice I learned: do not trust other people to do their jobs correctly. Make a nuisance of yourself to be sure stuff gets done, and if you can do something, then trust yourself to do it better than anyone else.

Now, after that small rant, we proceed to the physical side of the six-month mark.

Rather anticlimatically, there was nothing much all that surprising. My thighs, hips and chest were still increasing in circumference and I noticed more mass being deposited in the breasts. When I was at home, I did not put the same level of effort into my appearance as I did when I went outside, and I did not wear my breast forms. I could therefore see more definite projections starting to push out from the underside of my shirt. It was not much, but it was a start.

At this point, I reached the end of my course of laser hair removal treatment. While the hormones were helping soften the hairs on my face to a degree, this was only making it more difficult for the lasers, which require a colour contrast between the hair and skin, to pick out the already fair hairs that remained. My consultant and I believed there was no more to be done. The areas around the lips and chin were extra stubborn and were no longer responding.

I did alternative forms of hair removal, but they did not do enough to justify the effort at this time. I always found it difficult to go to these sessions for the need to present as male, my facial hair pushing me outside of the gender image I was trying to present. And I never liked spending the week prior growing out the hair just so it could be removed. I found this distressing, it limited my ability to make plans, and I loathed the constant feel of stubble. It made me feel like, for all my work, I was taking a huge step backwards and was still not the person I had spent so long dreaming and trying to be.

I still battle with this now and the continuing need for electrolysis in the perhaps vain hope of ridding myself of every piece of facial hair. I have not found an answer beyond waiting and hoping.

So, all in all, six months into the hormone treatment did not present any big physical changes, but it did mark some major administrative and lifestyle moments, such as my passport, starting the road to surgery and speech therapy, and quitting hair removal to instead focus on presenting more day-to-day.

All I then needed to do was sit back and let biology work its magic. Though, between you and me, I would not have minded if it could have gone a bit quicker.

Chapter Six

Nine-Month Review

What I first thought would be an incessant tumult of an unforeseen change and a lonely battle withstanding one obstacle after another, by the nine-month mark, had calmed more quickly and more substantially than I thought it would.

After years of constantly adapting to new situations, preparation, experimentation, and tiny but personal heroic stands, I had entered a period of transition where not much really happened. That being said, there were always small stories to tell, topics that might seem insignificant but which add together to form the conglomeration that is the transition. But before getting into that, what had hormones done to my body over those three preceding months?

If I am honest, not much.

It was a little underwhelming, I know, but things were chugging along, if only at a snail's pace. My hips were that bit wider than before and my waist that bit slimmer, my breasts incrementally more pronounced and my skin keeping its new luscious feel. So, physically, not much was in the works. Mentally, though, this was becoming a rather formative period. Hormones were doing something different to what I had come to expect.

I was still volatile, prone to flaring tempers, depressions and mania, and my libido was still shot full of holes. But what I did not anticipate was that I no longer felt any fear or apprehension about going outside, about being seen or heard. I had been afraid for so long I had forgotten what it was like to feel… perhaps not welcome, but at least tolerated with neither fanfare nor implicit opposition.

I may never escape the fact that I am transgender. It may continue to define me, my life and my interactions in subtle ways for as long as I live, but it was during this time that I began to see for the first time someone beyond the label that had ruled me for so many years. I started to omit the fact I was transgender from the conversation. I started to retreat into the cis role people assumed for me. And in my head, I became less and less transgender and more and more just another person out there in the world.

It was a weird feeling because it did not really feel like anything. Instead, it seemed a natural progression, the eventual acceptance into a world on whose gates I had been banging and pleading for entry. There was no sweeping relief nor uncontrollable satisfaction. It was more an absence of feeling, an absence of fear and uncertainty, an absence of scepticism and self-interrogation. It was being out in the world for a normal day, doing normal things, worrying about normal things and being treated as a normal person.

I might not yet have experienced my longed-for 'one day' but without the all-consuming label of 'transgender' dominating my view of myself, I was starting to see a path to which such a day might be possible.

In an earlier chapter, I raised the topic that at the start of my transition I had not wanted to be representative of the LGBT+ community. I did not want to be forced by my situation into the role of some kind of herald, to be defined solely by the label of 'transgender'. Defined, that is, by both society and myself. While that was still true to an extent, it was no longer as important to me. Being transgender was not a definition, a box in which to put myself and have to dictate my life. It was a stage gate, an enabler to living my own fuller life.

And I was starting to feel like I could.

I had another new job at this time where no one knew and most of those people with whom I interacted on a daily basis also did not know. I had reached a point where there were more people in my life that did not know, and not one of them batted an eye.

As I have mentioned before, it can be hard to be one hundred percent sure of how someone perceives you, whether they know or not simply by a look, but I was increasingly sure that they had no idea. And I knew because of how they acted to the chivalrous and slightly misogynistic cliches expected of them. Holding open the door for me, letting me cross the road, or saying something out of turn and then immediately reprimanding themselves because I was there. I was a woman to them and nothing more.

I was not only transgender.

That word was coming to mean less and less in the grand spectrum that formed my identity.

I was a woman.

I am a woman.

However, this did present me with a slight problem that, in my head, I wittily named The Mammary Barrier. Hormones were doing their job and my breasts were growing. It was slow, I will grant, but they were growing. This raised the issue of when and how I was going to stop wearing my breast forms.

I had a feeling it was going to be soon as it was becoming increasingly itchy, painful and uncomfortable to wear them. Most paradoxically, the heavyweight against my chest, which before had been a reassuring constant of my presentation, was now becoming oddly oppressive. It felt less like a vital part of my image and more like a cage holding me back from my full, free expression.

Regardless, the issue remained of how I was going to explain to my colleagues when I turned up one day having shrunk from a D-cup to an A-cup. Would I admit to being transgender, even though I did not want that word to hold such sway over me and I did not want to have to come out to a new group of people all over again? Or would I lie and spin some yarn about troubles during puberty? This was not technically incorrect, but perhaps a stretching of the truth. Or would I wait until a significant break and hope no one noticed upon my return?

I did not know what I was going to do at that point. It was something fast approaching and which I was aware I would have to tackle sooner rather than later. I needed to have a game plan. I thought I could use the recovery period from surgery to make the swap, but as I was going to learn, I was being far too optimistic about the surgery timeline and my own ability to have it.

But this does lead me to another topic. Less than a year into my hormone treatment, the surgery was now a fixed point on the horizon. In the gap between the six and nine-month mark, I had my first pre-surgery assessment. This was to check that everything was as they expected, decide whether electrolysis would be needed and formulate a plan forward.

Now, before I continue, the next section will contain some personal and graphic details regarding the site of the surgery. These details, however, may be useful for someone coming up to the same stage in their transition and wondering what will happen to them. I will therefore include them for completeness.

Ready?

I was circumcised in my teens for medical reasons. This normally precludes a straightforward surgery for the fact it removes some of the material the surgeon would otherwise use to make the new vagina. Due to this, they would need to use more skin from the scrotum and perineum, meaning these areas need to be removed of hair permanently before the surgery.

Upon initial inspection, they said I did not need to have any hair removed as the length of the penile shaft alone in my case gave them enough material to use. This would change, as the hormones would shrink the penis slightly over time, but if you have also been circumcised, do expect to face a similar hurdle. This will present an extra step before the surgery can go ahead, though with the waiting times as long as they are it is likely such treatment can be built into this period without affecting the final surgery window too much.

Though, when you go for your pre-assessment, be prepared. I had no notion myself of what this consultation would be like. No one had warned me or given me any indication. I went in thinking it would be a sit-down talk, discussing the road map and what was to come. I was wrong. Upon entering the examination room, the nurse told me to pull everything down and lie on the bed. The surgeon, clearly with very little time on their hands, strode in and looked over my prone, semi naked body. They prodded, poked, stretched, folded and thoroughly investigated the area of the coming surgery. All the while, they mused to themselves, said a few words, asked some questions about how I planned to use the vagina sexually, and then gave a brief summary of the next steps before departing. Barely five minutes had passed, but it felt a lot longer. Needless to say, it was uncomfortable and more than a little compromising. So, as I said, be prepared.

That being said, they were very professional and clearly understanding of the whole process. In my case, though I am not sure whether this will be universally representative, the hospital I chose was primarily a private medical centre, with the surgeon themselves operating in both the NHS and the private sector. This was a true mark of their skill, standing and experience in their field and one I had been advised to go for if I had the chance. The surgeon also specialised in those that had been assigned male at birth and had a shorter waiting this.

All this information is typically given to you to mull over during one of your appointments at the GIC. You then have time to research your choice of surgeon and come to a decision.

The clinic itself had a more exclusive feel than your standard hospital, and the entire wing, maybe even the floor, was dedicated to transgender patients during their recovery from the surgery. This would avoid any embarrassing or uncomfortable situations during such a time.

You will only be added to any waiting list once you have been referred to that surgeon by the GIC, which occurs after both the surgeon and the GIC have seen and approved you. This appointment is roughly two years after starting the hormone treatment, though there is always the possibility for further delays as the process is never straightforward. I also found that no one appears to talk to each other from all the various clinics and institutions. I was always having to backtrack and explain the steps I had been through every time I had an appointment or spoke to someone via phone or e-mail.

But maybe having now finished my hair removal treatments, if ultimately without complete success, and in that losing the final activity for which I presented as male, and with the prospect of my surgery on the horizon, was why I was starting to move away from the transgender label. My passport and driver's licence had come through. My parents were finally becoming accustomed to using my new name. Even my grandparents had accepted me at this point. Not only that, but I was the star grandchild after a successful Christmas. The fact I was transgender did not figure into any of this. I was presenting at work without worry. I was playing with my band in front of a crowd without worry. I was finally living without worry. I was finally just living.

And it was fantastic.

Chapter Seven

Twelve-Month Review

I had been on my hormone treatment for a year and this period of the transition was a little more eventful than usual.

There are several areas I want to cover. The first is the general physical update and how I changed my presentation to suit. I also began the group speech therapy sessions at the GIC, which deserves some discussion. And lastly, the hormones certainly made themselves known during this period, kicked into overdrive by stresses at work and to a level I had not experienced before. It was more than a little scary even more of the emotional stability upon which I had always implicitly relied while exciting to gain back control in other areas of my life. But all this I will get to soon enough.

Firstly, how were hormones changing my body?

It may not be exciting to write or read, but it was more of the same really. My hips were widening by that next tiny amount and my breasts developing in both size and sensitivity.

One odd thing I did notice, however, was that my nipples were becoming puffy. I cannot think of another way to put it except they looked as though they were being inflated from within. When they are stimulated and become erect, they instead shrink, the areola becoming small and more flush with the skin. They are still like this today, and having done some research into it, this can be normal for both transgender women and cis women as part of the breast's development and any significant hormonal change. For some, it simply stays around.

Still, I find it a little strange and am not overly fond of the way it looks, both naked and while wearing clothes. It can be fixed with surgery, but that seems like a drastic reaction to a small problem. For the most part, I suspect I will grow used to them in time, and I have found that some people prefer larger nipples anyway. And those who will even get to see them would be those who like me enough to see me in such a state. I would therefore hazard to say that they would have other things on their mind.

But the development in this area finally reached the point where I stopped wearing my breast forms. In work, with friends and in everyday life, I made the step to go all natural. It was a mixture of two things that made me choose this moment. The first was that my own breasts were becoming large enough to give some definition to clothes, even when wearing a coat. It was nothing drastic, but enough. And the second was that my forms now looked disproportionately large on me. I was becoming self-conscious about them being on the bigger end.

It was difficult that first day when I went outside without my forms. I had become so accustomed to that weight on my chest that it had become a kind of defence, a reassurance that I was presenting and living as a female. It had been there for three years, so when I saw my reflection without them it felt like I had lost something. I feared I had taken a big step backwards and people would see me for what I was not.

Yet, when I went out with friends without telling them I had made the change, they did not even notice. And when I was catcalled as much as usual, I realised that it did not matter. Society would see me a certain way, regardless of the size of my breasts. Instead, I decided to focus on what made me feel good, and at that stage, I felt better not wearing them.

To make the change at work, I decided to use an upcoming holiday as my chance. Two weeks away would hopefully give my colleagues a chance to forget what I looked like, so when I returned they would not notice that I was quite a lot smaller than before.

I could not wait.

Even though I had depended so much on my forms, being such an intrinsic part of how I identified, it always felt more by necessity than desire. They were a shield, a clue so people saw me the way I wanted to be seen. Removing that was scary. I would have to rely more on myself and my other qualities rather than the curves those bulbs of silicon could give me.

But being without them was liberating. I could present without the help they gave. I could wear what I wanted to wear without worrying about people glimpsing them. I could go without the types of bras they forced me to wear. And I realised that by taking this step I was more than enough on my own. I did not need them any more. I could just be me, with one less thing between me and the world, and that was a nice feeling.

Aside from the above, my skin was getting softer and the hairs about my body were fairer and growing more slowly. However, having stopped my laser treatments to remove my facial hair, I did not notice any reduction in that area from the hormones. Even now, I still shave around the lips and chin every other day and when the hairs do come through, they are bristly, if not very dark.

But with all the physical changes my body had been through, it was once again the mental that made the most impact.

I was no longer the same as I used to be. I was once blessed with a robust mentality, able to keep myself focused and in check when times became tough. I could point out the cause, determine the effect, create a plan to overcome it and then enact it. But over those months, a year into treatment, this became much more difficult and far less certain.

I was an ant, squirming beneath the focused emotions of my own hormonal sun, polarising me more often than not to the extremes of joy, rage, anguish and grief, and this was only becoming ever more evident as time went on. I found myself with the emotional volatility I had when I was in my teens, swinging from one extreme to the other, sometimes over the course of a day or even hours, except now I was being pushed by the surmounting stresses of adult life.

They carried me from tears to vitriolic rage and I could do nothing to stop them. And as much as I tried, there were times I could not even find a reason.

It could be something innocuous, or merely perceived, and I was gone, swept downstream to wherever my moods now took me. It was affecting everyday life to a greater degree than before. I was less receptive to others and quick to temper. I was more abrupt and more easily lost my focus. It was putting my job at risk and meant that, out in the world, I had to shield myself a lot more to prevent anything from setting me off. I could not think of any other plan to take.

I tried going to my GP but never got through. The service at work designed for this sort of thing required me to phone them up, which sparked my anxiety and vocal dysphoria. When I tried talking to my manager and HR about it – though I did not say what was causing the swings – they dismissed me and said I had to be focused at work and have the right attitude while in the office.

What then was I supposed to do?

I could only hope that the storm would ride itself out and that the holiday I was planning to take, and when I would divest myself of my breasts, would help me recentre. But after a lifetime of watching my emotions from a distance, studying them for my writing, analysing them, enjoying the good and circumventing the bad through rigour, strength and planning, I was thrown headfirst into a maelstrom for which I was wholly unprepared. I was overwhelmed and forced to do nothing but throw up whatever defences I could to keep myself on track. This was not a battle that could be won with logic.

Sadly, this is how my mind likes to work, even now. There was usually no origin to many of the incidents and for those where there were I was unsure whether I was overreacting or justified. Without a solid foundation, there was nothing to overcome, no plan to take beyond enduring this mad concoction of chemicals that lived on even after I did my best to fix the real world damage.

I was out of control and I was terrified.

Though, it was not all bad. There was some good.

I had recently joined the group speech therapy sessions at the GIC and at this point had so far had two classes. They gave me a checklist to pinpoint my strengths and weaknesses.

Not only was I able to test my voice in an environment where people and professionals could analyse it critically and propose improvements, but I could see other people at various stages and help them with those techniques I had found most helpful. My training in the theatre definitely came in use, not only making me comfortable to experiment with my voice, but knowing how to translate a particular sound into a physical movement and then explain it to others.

They also had a section dedicated to speaking over the phone, which would help me overcome part of that particular stumbling block, as well as public speaking and vocal projection while maintaining pitch and tone. I was hoping this would enable me to speak up in meetings at work, which could so easily run away from me, taken over by half a dozen forty-something salesmen all yammering to be heard. I needed all the help I could get with that job and work environment.

I had now been on my hormone treatment for a year, and, all in all, it was a mixed bag. Physically, everything was going according to plan, whereas mentally I would have been overjoyed at any semblance of a plan.

Chapter Eight

Fifteen-Month Review

Looking back at the previous chapters, it is surprising to me still how much can change in so short a span of time.

While physically I might have been doing well, I had been struggling with my mental stability, the stresses of adult life striking upon a body already imbibed on a fresh dose of teenage chemistry. I do not know whether it was personal growth, more balanced hormonal levels or a decreased load at work, or a combination of all three, but over the months since that one-year mark, I was doing better than I had in a long while.

I noticed more biological changes also. Where before they were mainly congregated in the hips, it was now moving up to the chest. My breasts were developing at an increasing rate and showing their substance more every day. They were still small, do not get me wrong, but they had a defined shape and I, at last, made the leap to stop wearing my breast forms in all situations.

I had trialled it out in the world, then with close friends and finally, after that holiday, at work. My plan was successful. No one commented and some of my friends did not even notice until I pointed it out. So, I came to the conclusion that it did not matter all that much and I could be just as happy and confident without them. And comfortable. It was quite literally a weight off my chest not having to wear those forms any more.

As a tip for this point of the process, when developing breasts are still too small for bras but have enough presence to press against clothing, I found that lace camisoles are a good middle ground. They hold everything together without feeling oppressive or oversized, though they can be warm to wear.

Aside from this, another change I noticed around this time was a slight increase in my libido. It was marginal, but it was there. While I was still not sexually active yet, it gave me hope that something I enjoyed before would not be gone forever.

That being said, without feeling the impetus to fulfil the need, I had not missed it. Sex had become a non-factor and, if I am honest, it was one less thing to worry about. But I did still wish that in the future I could reach a level where I could have and enjoy sex again, even if it would not be as large a part as it was before.

And the last physical change was around my face. The skin was getting even softer. I also noticed a slight change to the formation of my features, with rounder cheeks and the area beneath the eyes filling out, making them seem bigger and more circular. With my eyes, themselves seeming larger and my whole face appearing less angular, there was a feminine spark to them even before I put on my make-up. These changes were not so much that I looked like a different person, or would even be consciously noticeable by anyone else, but they added to the accumulation of subtle features that creates the image upon which is given the assumed social definition of a woman. It made me start to wonder whether I was coming to the point where I would no longer need my usual make-up routine to feel accepted out in the world.

I know it should not have been something upon which I needed to rely, but habits and stereotypes are hard to break. I had been doing my make-up before every trip outside for several years and it was as intrinsic to the image I had of myself as my forms used to be. It was a mask, a plate in my armour to protect me from the wandering eyes of those who would drag out the old and define me by that instead.

While I was sure I was not there yet, perhaps the time was coming. Certainly, I did not formulate the routine to the same stringent standards I used to do, making it more a formality than a mark of necessity. I was starting to believe that my features on their own would be enough for me to present as who I knew myself to be.

This brings me to the point I raised earlier about feeling the most secure and happiest I have in a while. It was because of this surety of my place in the world.

I was walking to work, minding my own business. I saw the familiar commuter faces, dodged cyclists and overzealous pigeons, and travelled by the war memorial and council-mandated tree surgeons. And I was just living life. Twelve to eighteen months before, this would have seemed impossible. Was this that unattainable 'one day' I had dreamed of having? Maybe, maybe not. The fever of the transgender still burned in my heart and made its mark upon my days, but I was closer now than ever.

Maybe it was a combination of all the reasons given over the course of these recent chapters, together encapsulating over a year of progress, but I think mostly it was a decrease in the stresses of life allowing me time to settle and see just how far I had come. I belonged in the world rather than having to prove my place through persistence or performance, and any stresses that did come my way were just part of the normal churn of life rather than core matters of identity.

The transition was one long boxing match. I was breathless in the corner of round forty-eight. The number of punches I had taken, the resistance I was forced to show and the number I gave in return built in me the foundation to tackle round forty-nine. Forty-nine made me strong enough for fifty, fifty for fifty-one, and ever onwards.

My footing was sure and I found a fearlessness brewing in my soul. I felt indomitable. I felt like I could go the distance.

The weird thing was that in hindsight it all seemed so easy. The hardship and heartache of those early days, the uncertainty and struggle that got me here became half-forgotten, just another bout I got through that could now be left behind. The battle was won in moments and the bell was close to being rung as a signal of my victory. Just as once you leave school you forget all those obscure algebraic laws and literary terms because you do not use them any more, it was the same here. I was forgetting the fight. Instead, I was living.

Chapter Nine

Eighteen-Month Review

A year and a half into the hormone treatment and it, at last, seemed that things were starting to calm down. The journey had plateaued and I had time to breathe and take stock. Thinking back, I find it difficult to believe how quickly it had all gone by, so much time parcelled up and consigned to the past. In memory, as in these pages, the months and all they held seem to just fall away. Days pass in a phrase and the moments that formed me spin upon a word. How can I capture each and give them their necessary weight? How do I do justice to the journey? I do not know if I can, but I hope that I can at least impart the essence, the soul, and let you feel the spirit of these years.

Most of the physical changes were becoming steadily less noticeable, though I was happy with the place they had reached, and the mental changes too were finally stabilising. Where just a few months prior I had been finding it difficult to control my emotions, them often running ahead of me even when I knew there was no logical reason, it was much easier now to keep myself together.

Each development was so minute that over the course of a month, they were almost invisible. If I had not been purposefully tracking them with the aim of consolidating them into a story of my transition, I doubt I would have remembered what it was like from one three-month window to the next and how much had happened in that time. It simply became the natural routine of life and it was nice to know that I had reached a place where the transition was no longer so disruptive or influential.

This period felt akin to The Wasted Years I wrote about earlier, in that it was another stretch of calm before something unknown and tumultuous. The surgery. That being said, however, due to the extent of the changes to my body, I ultimately decided against the idea of breast augmentation surgery.

After speaking with several women, both cis and transgender, I got the sense that contentment was easier to achieve by leaving them be rather than constantly battling to reach a kind of desired perfection. There was also the cost, the maintenance, the pain and recovery to consider, and I did not believe that these were justifiable in my case, because I was happy with what I had. I felt comfortable and could use the money I had saved to advance my other interests.

And I am content to this day. They are nothing stunning to be sure. My cleavage will never be the uplifted, barely contained ski slope of magazine covers that attract buyers to the shelf, but they are average and they are mine, and they do the job they are meant to do to the letter.

Yet there was still the matter of my other surgery. Whereas that first set of wasted years was also spent on a waiting list, the time had been mine with which to experiment and find my ideal path forward, whether it be to transition, how and to what extent. Now, all I could do was sit and muse over what path through surgery to take. There were three choices as I saw them.

1) To not have the surgery.
2) To have the full surgery, the vaginoplasty.
Or 3) a middle ground, the labiaplasty.

Either of the latter two is a final choice, and once done they cannot be undone, and one cannot be transformed into the other.

I had been wishing for the surgery for so long that it was inevitable it would happen, and that I would never want anything else. And I was tired of the old thing getting in the way and always serving as a reminder of the distance that yet remained between me and my desired gender. But which type of surgery was best?

The way I thought about it was that the vaginoplasty was a full bore, future-proofed solution but with a far higher initial investment of pain, discomfort and risk. With several weeks of hospitalisation followed by months of home recovery, would it be worth it? And while the labiaplasty would not be as invasive or painful, if I ever became sexually active again, then that would restrict what I was able to do and enjoy. As I was then, I could not see myself having sex in the near future due to the effect hormones were having on me, but I was hopeful that I would do so again. This would settle and then who knew what might happen?

In the end, I did not reach a decision at that point. I was hoping that an upcoming consultation at the GIC would have helped, but due to the ever-increasing cuts to the NHS – and this was all before *Covid* only made things worse – waiting times increased yet again, even for someone so far into the process as I was. This meant I was not likely to speak to someone until the following year at the earliest.

I, therefore, became resolved that if the years looked as though they were starting to slip by, I would do this final step through the private healthcare system. It would be costly, but I was fortunate to have my parent's blessing and support for this decision. Though it had taken some adjustments to get us to where we were now, they had been with me from the beginning. And I do believe that we are closer now as a family because of what we have been through together these past few years. So, the wait continued. The everlasting, interminable, indefinable wait, with each day easier than the one before.

I know this is not the most enticing or engaging reading and there are few words of dramatic wisdom, but I guess that is the nature of the slow epilogue. When all the trials have been fought, victories attained and peace manifested, the story does not end. Life must go on with the consequences of what was done. They yawn back to normality.

Nonetheless, I am glad that I was able to reach such a place. Throughout the entire process, I have been incredibly fortunate, but even then, there were times I doubted that there could be any lasting joy in the path I had chosen. I feared it would be a lifelong struggle. But no, the tumult was approaching its end and life felt like it could be mine for the making. If I could have gone back and told my twenty-one-year-old self anything, it would have been that: "Yes, it is achievable."

Chapter Ten

Twenty-One-Month Review

How did I get here?

Even though I had not yet reached anything near an ending, I sometimes thought back to those moments at the start of all this when I was still contemplating everything I was feeling and what it meant. People often ask me how long my transition has been and when it was I knew. There is some truth to the answer that I always knew, at least retrospectively. Understanding the existence of gender dysphoria and the transition made sense of so much of my youth that I wonder if this outcome was destined from the start and if it was just a matter of when and how. But there are a few concrete moments that stand out to me as defining. Summer 2015 was one of those moments.

It was when I was in Edinburgh performing as part of the Fringe Festival. I was presenting as male most days during that period. While I dressed occasionally, it was once or twice a week for nights out or days where there was no other major commitment. Even though I knew I would hate it, I agreed to grow a beard for that show, as if to force myself through a test by contradiction.

This beard would trap me as male for the months it would take to grow as well as the several weeks we were to perform. And I hated it. There is no surprise there, but the extent of my loathing did shock me. It was hot, and itchy and I wanted to rip the blasted thing right off my face, even if it should take my own skin with it. Being confined to a form that was not my own was strangely liberating because, standing on the Royal Mile in the rain, handing out flyers, I knew this was not me. I had an answer. There was something wrong deep inside, and going on the journey to come was the best chance I had of figuring it all out.

But what strikes me about that is just how much had happened since then. So many uncertain nights, so much happiness, sadness, fear and joy. There were points of resolution followed by a series of daunting challenges. It is impossible to recall it all. Even in the process of writing this book, I am sure there is another tome's worth I have omitted through senility. And if I had not kept this record, I doubt in another five years I could accurately relate just how long and arduous yet ultimately rewarding the transition has been.

Perhaps like a trauma, my mind was trying to protect me by selectively forgetting the most painful moments, purposefully omitting large portions of my life for the undercurrent of stress and anxiety they contained. Or maybe because this late in the game there was no longer the barrage of new experiences or wars to outlast. They were instead replaced by long gaps of just living life, of routine, the tossing and turning diminished to blips within month after month of idle contentment.

Maybe that was the ultimate validation. I had been through the fire and come out the other side hardened, tempered and reforged into something that a bearded individual on the Royal Mile could never have imagined. All going well, I would live more years as the person I was than what I used to be, and even more than the gauntlet through which I passed to get here. That would be my reward. The hurdles to come would be the standard affair of a modern, adult life, and having come through all this, even though I struggled to remember it all, I knew that in having overcome it, I could not now be stopped. It would take something serious to match those last few years.

Life, though, would find a way.

Because there was the final battle to fight, that of my surgery. I had another appointment booked at the GIC in early 2020, meaning that by extrapolating and having everything go to plan, my surgery would be roughly two years after starting my hormone treatment. It would be another round of pain, agony, uncertainty and ultimate recovery, a last boss for which these years had prepared me. And if nothing else, it would have given me something to write about.

So, for now, that was it. Another three months are gone and another three to go. Another chapter. Another milestone in which was confined a life passing in thoughts. But as difficult or as impossible as things might have seemed at any given time, it was only a transitory hardship.

There would come many years to forget even more of it but carry forward the strength it imbued. I could get through this and there would be joy waiting for me on the other side in a form I could never have pictured. A couple years traded for a lifetime. Come the end, I would look around at everything I had managed to build and not realise how I got here. But it would be me, it would be mine. It would be strong, and it will be beautiful.

Chapter Eleven

Twenty-Four-Month Review

Two years on hormones and a surprising amount had happened and gone wrong, since my previous touchstone.

The first was an update regarding the GIC and my surgery. While I was successfully referred to my chosen surgeon, by the time the first *Covid* lockdown in March 2020 closed much of the UK, the referral had not yet been received, meaning no date had been allocated. That limbo looked set to persist for many months but I was still hopeful for the surgery to occur within the year. I would not have been so optimistic had I known just how big a part of our lives *Covid* would become.

However, the prospect of the surgery remained real, a fixed point that was delayed but nonetheless inevitable. I had given a lot of thought to the surgery and even more so while things were otherwise waylaid, and I made the decision to go with the full vaginoplasty. Even though this would be more invasive, painful, and risky and would require a lot of post-operative care, I decided on the future-proofed solution. While I was not that sexually active at the time, I was in a polyamorous relationship that offered me the freedom to take the time I needed to rediscover my libido. I did not feel pressured into it as I knew the other members of the polycule could get from each other what I was unable to offer at that time. That being said, my libido was coming back slowly. Speaking to people who had had the operation, they said that things picked up afterwards and everything worked as it was supposed to. So, I kept my fingers crossed.

At the same appointment where I was referred to my surgeon, the consultant told me that the dose of my hormone treatment needed to be increased. A recent blood test showed that my oestrogen levels were not where they needed to be. This irked me somewhat, I must admit. I had been having regular blood tests, two to three a year, since I was initially prescribed my hormones, and I had no idea why it took them so long to notice the levels were not where they were supposed to be. Had this caused even more delays to my transition than I had already experienced? I do not know, but part of me still wonders if I could have had in one year what had so far taken me two if they had noticed sooner.

So, for anyone going through the transition, I recommend calling up the clinic a couple of weeks after any blood test to see if there is an action that needs to be taken.

Thankfully, the update to my dosage came through just before they locked down my local GP and they were able to sort it all out for me. Yet, this increase in dose did cause a resurgence of some of the less desired side effects.

I began the increased dosage before the prescription came through, while I was still working from the office, and all the old emotional instability returned in force. The magnifying glass flared both good and bad moods, swinging from one to the other without prediction. This was not helped by some serious public transport failings during the same period. It took all my resolve to keep myself going. Maybe I could have acted differently, and been in contact with my work's HR department to see what dispensation could be made for me, but I did not. Instead, I took the option for reduced hours to allow time for self-care. This did help, but it meant I was not earning as much.

Perhaps I should have put more pressure on all my employers to help me when I needed it rather than being victim to the whims of corporate fate. I am good at my job, regardless of what it is, and they would surely want to keep me working. What would they do to make that so? And it could only be a positive change to normalise the daily issues transgender individuals face in a work environment that might not even occur to someone on the outside. It would help them improve their policies while giving me the support I needed.

But I kept my head down instead and carried on.

Typical of me, really.

Anyway, aside from the mental turmoil, the increased dose also kickstarted some more physiological changes. My hips were widening, my shoulders shrinking, my breasts growing larger and other feminine areas becoming more pronounced. It would take several months to a year to fully realise, as the delay in noticing my low levels of oestrogen had likely put me behind the typical timeline I outlined earlier in this book. Yet, I was oddly grateful for the quarantine at this point. Working from home allowed me to take life at my own pace and not have to worry about commuting or the office. And with this new set of changes banging on my door, it was best that they happen now when I had the luxury of time.

One obstacle did present itself, but it steered me in a direction I should have resolved long ago. When I was at the referral appointment I mentioned above, the doctor asked me why I wanted the surgery. I almost had to fluff the answer as I had not given it too much thought. It was a foregone conclusion to me. It had to happen because it was always going to happen. It was just a part of the transition and what transgender people did, so I thought at the time. Because of that, I had never really examined why.

Then, a few weeks after that appointment and just before lockdown fully hit, I was chatting with a friend and that part of my current physiology was acknowledged without warning and in a context that threw up alarms I had not heard in a year or more.

That gave me pause. I had to figure out why. Why would a part of my body that was not even functional, did not represent me and whose days were numbered hold such sway over me? Why would someone even acknowledge that it existed and how they would like to use it – admittedly without consenting with me that this was a discussion I wanted to have – send me tumbling back through age-old dysphoria?

I spent a lot of time thinking about it and I came to understand that as long as it was there, it was an anchor to an old biology, the lone last vestment of the body that was there before the transition began. I had come a long way since then, and in every objective sense I had taken my identity far beyond what this thing represented. Yet subjectively, it was a lifeline to what I once was and kept alive the memory of that person. It would therefore continue to shape how others would see me once they knew it was there.

With it, they would think there were certain actions I would be able to take and therefore want to make. They would use it to define me by what they thought it represented, how it mattered to them and how it informed me in their eyes, rather than how I tried to represent myself through every other tool I possessed. It could so easily matter more than everything else combined. My internal identity and external representation were no longer aligned. I was what others chose to see, not what I now was. I was no longer living my life, my own little part of the world, but I was once again expected, dictated, powerless.

Malformed.

And for that reason, it had to go.

I needed to cut this anchor loose. It might have been the last five percent needed to make me whole, but it only took one chip in the portrait, one access for judgement, or one bad day to undo years of progress.

Chapter Twelve

Twenty-Seven-Month Review

Quiet. Waiting. Limbo. Once again this was the state of the transition, rocked from madness and tumult into stale and sterile boredom. This was mostly due to continued lockdowns at the time, so most of my struggles were related to work and isolation, and everything to do with the transition took a back seat.

I was on the books to have surgery during 2020, but my referral from the clinic had of course been delayed so it was looking like 2021 might be the year. Maybe? Perhaps? Who knew at this point? I chased and pushed as much as I could but was stonewalled at every turn. Readjusting my expectations had been difficult, but I was resigned to it now. The thing I kept telling myself was that all going well, I would have many more years post-surgery than there were spent waiting for it.

Aside from that, most of the dramatic changes hormones kicked up in recent months had now ceased. My skin and body hair had become as soft as it seemed it would. My mood had stabilised, on the whole, and I was able to work through any tough spots with my usual bag of tricks. Fat redistribution had also stopped and the figure

I was left with appeared to be my final form. I was starting to really like the way my body was looking.

But there were two things that were still trucking along. Due to the recent increase in my dosage, my breast development shot up to another level. While I did not and probably never would have breasts large enough for a *Playboy* photoshoot, they were definitely growing and in short order reached a level that worked well with my figure. Though my nipples were once again doing that weird puffy thing they had been for the past couple of months.

At first, I was not sure what this was and was a little self-conscious about it – actually, I still am, even now – but after doing a little research I found that it is just a natural part of breast development. It normally comes in tandem with any major hormonal change, for which I definitely qualify, and usually occurs in the second to last stage of breast growth, with the limits of the puff being the outer perimeter of where the breasts will grow. Of course, this is for cis-women during their natural puberty, but it gave me hope that not only will my nipples settle down but that my breasts would also grow some more and make up for the time lost when my dosage was too low to stimulate the necessary growth.

Looking back on this now, however, while my breasts did grow a little more over the following months and years, my nipples did not calm as I had hoped. Though, a quick look online showed several clinics that do simple reduction surgeries. Taking less than an hour and done under local anaesthetic, they can permanently fix such issues. I will continue to ponder whether this is something I do in the future, but for now, I was happy enough with the outcome. My body had reached a shape that made me content to see myself in the mirror.

The second of the two major changes was my libido. Over the last year or so, I had been noticing a rhythmic cycle in my libido tracking with my testosterone-blocking injections. As this hormone was the key driver of my libido before my treatment, it made sense that as it would start to bubble up in the weeks leading up to an injection, so would my libido. This would then correspondingly plummet after the injection. However, if I were to plot this rise and fall on a graph, there would be a steady trend upward, with each peak being larger than the one before. This was becoming even more obvious after my oestrogen dosage was increased, which may have been filling in the gap left behind by the lack of testosterone.

So, I waited to see what would happen after the most recent injection and how drastic it was compared to those that had come before. While there was a drop, it was interesting to note that before the injection, my libido was perhaps the highest it had been since I started my hormone treatment and the drop did not make as large a dent as I thought it would. It might have been the unusually hot summer we were having at the time, but my libido remained pretty active even in the immediate aftermath of the injection.

This gave me hope that as the months went on, it would continue to rise and that after my surgery when the injections would no longer be needed, it would settle at a serviceable level. Because I did miss sex. I had been more than two years without it at this point. My appetite was there, but my body was taking its time catching up. I felt it starting to rile, and I just had to keep my fingers crossed that little while longer.

Chapter Thirteen

Thirty-Month Review

Life can sometimes be storybook, and not always in the best of ways. It has its ebbs and its flows and I felt like I was in the beginning stages of something of a finale, at least for this chapter of my transition. I had been on hormones for two and a half years at this point and most of the physical changes, it seemed, had settled down. There were still subtle shifts towards a more feminine physique, but most of the major effects had finished playing their parts and the rest was more about increments asymptotically tending towards finality.

For that reason, this was when I decided to stop documenting my treatment as the slow epilogue had decayed below background levels and the half-life just kept ticking on. I wanted instead to focus on the future, because this period of the transition had been unusually active, despite the fact we were still a country beset by a virulent pandemic.

The first piece of action was a resurgence in my attempts at hair removal. Seeing as there was a virus out there that had significantly changed the social dynamic, making it preferable to wear a mask when going outside, I had an idea.

I had stopped my laser facial hair removal shortly into my hormone treatment as it was interfering too much. Not only did I have to present as male on those days when I went in for the appointment, but I had to let the hair grow for several days to a week beforehand, so the specialist had something to work on.

Now that had changed. With a mask, I was able to live as normal when I did go outside even while I was letting what little facial hair I had left grow out unseen. So, I resumed the removal treatment, this time opting for epilation at a salon whose owner was a friend of mine and knew about my situation. As such, I could present however I wished and rely on the mask to cover that which no one but they needed to see.

After a few sessions, I noticed a temporary improvement, especially on the jawline and the horn of the chin. It was becoming sparser and taking longer to grow back, but it was still as persistent as before once it did. The upper lip and the patch below the bottom lip were once again proving the most stubborn. Either way and despite the fact these treatments were some of the most painful things I had ever had to endure, I was glad to be making progress again on something I thought I would be stuck with for the rest of my life.

Aside from that, *Covid* was continuing to delay my efforts for surgery, but since the previous chapter, my referral letter came in from the GIC and I had my second pre-operation consultation with the surgeon. Annoyingly, they changed their mind and decided that I would need hair removal down there after all, so they could use the extra pieces of skin. It would only add a few more months to the road map and, if nothing else, would provide something interesting to talk about in what was going to become the third section of this book.

However, the most startling thing to come out of that appointment was a profound sense of terror.

Not only did the surgeon talk through the operation, postcare treatment and some of the risks, but I was given all the booklets, leaflets, pamphlets and other informational pieces that covered everything about the operation in detail. Reading them, I was suddenly struck by the sense that this was no longer a distant abstraction, a mere administrative test for something far in the future, but something that was very much real. It was happening and now loomed large on the horizon.

It would be a staggering change to life and body, incur pain and difficulty, and carry with it no small risk of adverse side effects. And these side effects, as well as the length of the post-operative recovery, were something I did not know fully going in. There had not been a lot of people to talk to about it and all this new information was making me question whether it was something that was worth doing.

For me, the transition was ninety-five percent done at this point. For the most part, I was happy with the results. So, was it worth going through such hardship and risk for something that may, in the end, only result in a marginal improvement to my outlook and a general sense of dysphoria? And some of these risks truly terrified me. Hair regrowth. Infection. Dead tissue. Prolapse. A fistula between the anus and vagina. Possibility for a colostomy bag. Lacklustre aesthetics. Loss of orgasms. Immediate and lasting pain. The constant, uncomfortable maintenance of vaginal dilation.

So, what should I do?

Should I stop? Would that cut me off from the NHS route? Or do I keep going and accept the risks and pain for the possible good that would come years on from the surgery itself?

In the end, I did what I always do when I was faced with a hard decision. I made a list of pros and cons. Each one I weighed on a scale from one to three based on how important it was. Even giving my fear of the side effects a massive five out of three for how much they scared me, the pros won out.

I was going to do it. I had made up my mind.

The list had decreed it.

While I was comfortable with who I was, that was in a working-from-home setting, rarely going outside and only seeing close friends and family. Thinking back to the before-times, I remembered the constant doubt and unsettled feeling that came from knowing I was not finished. This was not just for all the reasons I mentioned a few chapters prior, but for everything else I had not considered, not yet experienced, and all that could be possible once I was finally made whole.

I was going to do it. I had made up my mind.

The list had decreed it.

It was the next big step and would round off my journey nicely with the third and final part of the transition. Thus, with little fanfare, jubilation or even resolution, I had reached a second finale. The slow wait of hormones was at an end and I was bracing for another set of monumental upheavals, another set of drastic alterations to self, life and livelihood.

But then, it was just one more near-insurmountable obstacle to overcome. What of it, right? I had come through enough already that another should not be too much trouble. This would be an end and a beginning. An end of the transition and the beginning of the rest of my life. All I had to do was make it past one final precipice.

That was all I had to do…

Part Three

The Edge of a Knife
The Surgical Transition

Chapter One

Demons, Dysphoria, and Imposter Syndrome

When I was first going through the transition, it had always been my fixed end goal to undergo surgery. It was there on the horizon, a looming, incontestable precipice. While I did not, for reasons I will explain in their own dedicated chapter, I nonetheless went quite far through the process and came to learn a lot. Thus, it seems only right that I should continue my transition in the hypothetical, at least for the moment, to complete this stage of the journey for anyone who goes further than I did.

There is a myriad of options, starting from non-gender-related cosmetic surgeries, but below are the main operations that deal with gender reassignment. These may make you feel uncomfortable. They are new and personal, scary and life-altering, but I suggest you research them independently to know all you can about the operations that may be in your future. It will be a big step and a lot of mental preparation will be required. There are risks and side effects to all and a considered approach must be taken, weighing the positives against the negatives for your particular situation. I had it in the plan for nearly four years and even then, the prospect of it made me cross my legs, queasy at the thought of the change and pain. But if surgery is your dream, as it used to be mine, then with it your journey might finally be over.

Life can continue, pure and of your making.

List of Common Gender Reassignment Surgeries

Operation	*Assignment*	*Summary*
Breast Augmentation	AMAB	Often called 'top surgery', this is the enlargement and/or shaping of the breasts. It is a common procedure done by many transgender women as hormone therapy normally produces a lower cup size than closely related cis-women. This is not covered by the NHS but can be done privately for around £5,000–£6,000.
Mastectomy	AFAB	Similarly called 'top surgery', this is the

		removal of the breasts and breast tissue, creating a more male-contoured chest. This is covered by the NHS but can only occur after a period of HRT.
Vaginoplasty	AMAB	Known as 'bottom surgery', this is the creation of a functional vagina by inverting the penis and using the scrotum and surrounding skin to form the vulva, with the glans becoming the clitoris. This is covered by the NHS, but requires hair removal and carries significant risks.
Labiaplasty	AMAB	This is another form of 'bottom surgery'. It instead produces the surface detail of a vagina without

creating the internal structure. It is less invasive and carries fewer risks, but is not functional in the same way and cannot be used for sexual intercourse. It is covered by the NHS, but once one is chosen, it cannot be changed after the fact.

Metoidioplasty/ Phalloplasty	AFAB	Also called 'bottom surgery', this is the creation of an erectile prosthetic phallus through either shaping the expanded clitoris from hormones (M) or skin grafts from the stomach and thighs (P). This is covered by the NHS, but is also invasive and carries risks, requiring long

recovery times. It can occur in two separate operations with a period of waiting in between.

Hysterectomy	AFAB	Removal of the uterus with a further option to remove the fallopian tubes if necessary or desired.
Facial Feminisation Surgery	AMAB	Feminising cosmetic surgeries that modify bone or cartilage structure, typically in the jaw, brow, forehead, nose and cheek areas to feminise the facial features. This is not covered by the NHS and can cause swelling and drastically alter one's appearance beyond desired bounds.

Vocal Feminisation Surgery	AMAB	This procedure is to artificially alter the range or pitch of a person's vocal cords. It is not covered by the NHS and the procedure carries the significant risk of permanently changing or impairing your voice in a manner not desired.

There are many other surgeries, such as tracheal shaving or buttock augmentation, but those listed above are the most common and deal almost exclusively with a gender transition. I recommend researching each and asking your consultant when you get the chance, and budgeting appropriately. The gender transition is not cheap and will require thousands of pounds even in the best case, and vastly more if you decide to seek private treatment.

Now, I was planning for this section to form the concluding part of what would be the trilogy of the transition, a series that tracked my journey to and out from under the surgeon's knife. I had a while to go before I got that far, but as you might already have guessed by the relative brevity of the coming pages, things did not go according to plan. Yet some of the groundwork had already been laid, so it was time for me to try my hand at this whole surgery business.

As with the rest of the book, this will get personal by its very nature, both emotionally and physically. You have been warned.

We begin here where we left off. Appointments, leaflets, information, terror and running down the clock.

As I said, the list had decreed it. It was no longer a choice but was instead in the hands of fate, the predestined endpoint of the transition. It was just what was always supposed to happen.

Now, though, came the matter of hair removal around the site of the surgery. The basic form of the surgery is to invert the penile shaft so that the glans become the clitoris, with the skin of the penis, scrotum and perineum becoming the inside lips of the vagina. This means they need to be clear of hair otherwise they will continue to grow on the inside, causing issues and possible infection later down the line. But this step was once more hindered by the various quarantines of 2020.

Even though it would be a while before I would start my treatments, I experienced some of the administrative steps. A few weeks after seeing my surgeon for the second pre-operative consultation, I was e-mailed a collection of letters that, I believed, formed part of the application the specialist submits to the NHS funding agency to fund my hair removal treatment. I forwarded all of these to my specialist just in case they needed them. I was told they would then apply for this funding after they had had a chance to see me, as they would need to estimate the number of sessions and the total time and cost.

I was waiting for my funding to be approved, but due to the pandemic, I expected this to either take a while or fall through completely. As such, I reached out to my specialist and learned that, if push came to shove, I could pay for it myself.

Regarding the specialist themselves, the GIC has a list of all those that are qualified, but you can also search for them yourself using the BIAE (British Institute and Association of Electrolysis) website. You can filter its members by those qualified for pre-SRS hair removal, which is the type required for the surgery in question, and then contact them yourself to get the ball rolling. You will also be required to liaise with them in the first instance to get sessions booked and the treatment started. The GIC will not do this for you.

While I had not yet had any treatment, I had spoken to my specialist and found them to be kind, understanding, and clearly knowledgeable. I trusted them to do a good job and treat me with the necessary sensitivity once we were finally permitted to have an appointment.

Because this was yet another period of incessant waiting. It would have been better had the entire world not decided to close its doors in unison due to *Covid*, but after ten months in lockdown, my emotions were starting to strain along with my patience. I could work from home but as such had little reason to go anywhere except out of necessity, even when the rules were relaxed and we were allowed. I saw my partner about once per week or fortnight, otherwise, I spent most of my time completely isolated. This was as enlightening as it was difficult. In the weeks and months trapped inside, gender dysphoria became my own personal plague.

Spending so much time inside by myself meant that I did not present as much anymore, if at all, to the level I did before. I mostly dwelt in my flat, wearing pyjamas more often than not. This was part of the lockdown curse, but there was no motivation to do anything else. No friends. No rehearsals. No gigs. In this guise, I noticed that my own self-image, how I perceived myself, was steadily changing, reverting from the feminine-style presentation I had cultivated in the before-times and towards a more natural, foundational state.

As I had not finished the hair removal, both on the face and elsewhere, when left untended, my body still showed signs of its prior configuration. Over time, these became the norm and started to assert themselves once more as fact, increasing the distance, in my mind, between where I was and where I wished to be. I no longer saw myself as a woman but a mutant creature stuck somewhere between, even after all this time when I had thought myself so near completion.

This caused a rather large, self-destructive spiral from which I did not emerge for several months, and only then after returning home to stay with my parents, shutting off all social media, and focusing on a dramatic exercise routine. Until then, I was a volcano of bitterness, depression, and self-loathing.

The slightest setback could set off a chain reaction of negativity, like I was still playing catch-up to an ever-receding aspiration, failing to meet the most basic expectations of my desired gender. I believed I would never fit the standard held for me. My mind cannot help but compare myself to the effortless femininity of cis women and how lacking I am in comparison. And after working so hard, putting in so much effort for so long, to still feel like this was heartbreaking.

This was, and still is, especially keen in a polyamorous relationship. I put myself alongside other partners and found myself wanting like I did not deserve to be in their company, nor stack up to warrant the mantle of 'girlfriend'. In my darker moments, my brain whispered that not only was I not worthy but that I never would be.

What then was the point of even trying if there was no chance of success? Was despair finally allowed if I knew with surety the subpar outcome of the road on which I had set myself? To be a stereotype of my desired gender felt like an unreachable aspiration and that I should not even bother any more. I was little more than an imposter in a set of skin not my own, appropriated and never to be finished.

I sought help, but even today these wounds still fester.

Chapter Two

Liberation and Administration

Much of the transition is a play of two acts, a division of labour that splits life into halves. The first are the administrative challenges and practical matters, and the second are the personal and emotional elements that stem from all these consequences, both known and unknown.

Let us start with the practical side.

After over a year of querying and back and forth e-mails, I finally got my first appointment with the electrolysis specialist for my pre-surgery hair removal. Several things of note emerged from this process.

After the second visit to my surgeon, I was tasked to find my own local specialist using the site I mentioned in the previous chapter. This was done using the paperwork I received from the hospital, though I was told by my specialist that they were missing some of the forms they needed to send off the funding application. I chased everything up from the hospital and, after several months of pestering, eventually got everything that was required.

So, for future reference, you get two lots of documents. The first is called the PPN documentation, which is a series of letters of proof detailing the treatment needed and giving the necessary authorisation. The second is another letter, an information sheet and, most importantly, a quotation sheet. While both lots of documents are required, it is the quotation sheet that is the most crucial. The specialist needs this to apply for funding to commence the treatment.

It took about eight months for me to receive the first batch of forms and a further three months to get the second, though this all took place during the pandemic, which likely delayed things. There were then further issues, as the appointment itself had to wait until restrictions allowed it. But with all that said, it finally happened and I could experience yet even more hair removal in all its joyous agony! To date, I have had epilation, laser removal and electrolysis on my face, with the pain of each, ranked in that order.

I had not yet had electrolysis done on the surgery's donor site, as my first session with the specialist was an examination and introduction to the course. They used this to determine how many sessions I would need and therefore how much money to request from the NHS funding agency.

I also learned several key pieces of information. First is that the donor site was a little bigger than I expected and they required about two millimetres of growth to enable treatment. Their advice was to shave about a week or two before the session and then let it grow. Second was that once sessions start, they take place weekly and then taper off as the hair starts to dissipate. And lastly was about anaesthetic. I was not aware, but it was highly recommended that I get anaesthetic cream to use on the area before the electrolysis session as it was apparently going to be ludicrously painful otherwise.

I was pointed towards EMLA Cream, which can be bought over the counter at any pharmacy, though it is not common so it may need to be ordered. If you explain it is for hair removal, that should be enough to convince them of the need.

Now we can move on to the more personal part of this stage of the transition. Quarantine had lasted for fourteen months at this point and things were on the mend, at least for the moment, meaning I had more commitments taking me outside. After so long, it was quite a change. But I did notice something rather dramatic, something that was a pleasant improvement from how I had felt over the winter prior and what formed the bulk of the chapter before. While dysphoria was still an issue, I made great strides in dealing with it, and I also determined its source. It came down to two main aspects.

Body and presentation.

I spent a lot of time over those months exercising. I bought an indoor bike to use in the flat over lockdown, so I could work out without risking breaking any restrictions and do so while watching a film or playing a game. I also began doing a series of callisthenics, stretches and other resistance exercises. All this together drastically improved not only my health and my figure but how I perceived myself. Perhaps it was the physical improvements themselves or maybe it was actually getting out of my pyjamas for a while, but more and more I was seeing myself as female regardless of how I dressed. I was coming to like again what I saw in the mirror.

Amazingly, it was consistent. Only rarely did this falter, mainly when I had to grow out my facial hair ready for another bout of hair removal. To like my body unreservedly for the first time in months, perhaps years, with no operations or additions, was an astounding relief. I felt like I did not need to worry about it anymore and could simply get on with the business of living.

And in presentation, having been inside for so long, the routine I used before lockdown no longer applied. I did not put on my make-up daily and had not done so for a while, saving it mainly for special occasions. But I also found myself keeping it off while heading to the shops and using a mask to cover the rest of my face. It was like a trial run, to have just my eyes clear of make-up and see if anyone cared.

They did not.

So, like the good scientist that I am, I experimented more. I repeated this and again found that no one gave me a second look. The next step was then to go out without the mask or make-up, and I did this while I was with my partner for support. I felt a little uncomfortable, but I drew scant attention if any. And last but not least was to then go out alone with neither mask nor make-up. After having had my hair cut so I felt a little more groomed, I popped to the shops to top up my electricity meter, and I felt good. Not only did I not get any looks or side-eye comments, or people twigging the fact I was transgender, but I felt free.

Just... free.

It is hard to describe just how big a step this was for me. From the start, I remember saying to my friends that I would one day like to go outside and live a day without having to spend an hour at the make-up table curating my appearance beforehand. It was exhausting and time-consuming, but it also defeated the point, in a way, of trying to be me. As with my breast forms, it was just another layer between me and the world. I hated the fact that I felt like it was necessary for me to be accepted. But now I no longer needed it. I could go without it and instead, use make-up to enhance my features for those occasions that warranted it. Then, for the rest of the time, I could just be me.

I could just be me...

Chapter Three

Doubt

The true core of life is that it can sometimes be a tragic farce that takes you places you never wanted to go, but having gone has led you to where you needed to be. And again, we play the game of two halves. The first was a simple matter of administration, the hair removal funding was lost somewhere in the bureaucratic ether due to *Covid*, while the second was a period of harrowing illness and unasked for enlightenment.

Both, in their own ways, made me question the path I had set for myself and whether putting myself in the hands of fate, a predetermined desire based upon a list and a dream more than five years out of date was now the right choice for me.

This will be painful and embarrassing to write, but that is the modus operandi of this book, and kind of the point when it comes down to it. While this book should never be considered a single point of reference for a spectrum that encompasses an infinite variety of stories and identities, it should serve instead to break the ice of a narrative few get to hear and to tell in ink what need not be asked of anyone ever again.

The illness that made me question myself was an infection that found its way to my bladder and that then became resistant to the initial load of antibiotics. They eventually managed to clear it up with stronger medication, which itself caused a heap of unpleasant side effects, but in the months, I was suffering, I broke. Physically and mentally, I simply shattered. And the focus of this incessant torture was the area of my body that was soon going to be the site of my surgery. It was as though I had a glimpse into what it could be like should the operation go wrong, or what the recovery might be like even should it go well. And there was no telling if this surgery would only make the pain I was currently feeling worse.

It was a brutal period full of anguish, discomfort, tears, fear and paranoia. All in all, it took ten months for me to see the end of what this one infection did to me.

The damage the infection did to my bladder was severe, stripping away the naturally protective lining and causing a condition called interstitial cystitis. This is a continued and repeated inflammation of the bladder and uncontrollable activation of the surrounding muscles.

For the first five months, I was in agony and felt the constant, desperate need to go to the toilet. Day and night, it haunted me. Every minute of every hour it cut through every other thought and feeling, stopped me from working and kept me from sleeping for more than an hour at a time. I spent over eight months without one uninterrupted night and even tried to sleep on the toilet as it was the only place

I could relax. My diet was slashed to avoid any food or drink that could set me off. I went to the hospital twelve times in total, twice to A and E desperate for help when I did not know what was happening to me, once in an ambulance after the side effects nearly claimed my life, three times for diagnostic operations and procedures, and six times for unpleasant treatments that often caused panic attacks. I self-harmed by trying to smash my head through the bathroom door when I would not stop going, and when spasm-induced incontinence kept me rooted to the seat for hours on end.

I truly thought about ending my life.

And everything added together crippled my ability for creativity, strained my relationship, fostered a routine of idleness and apathy as a way just to get through the day, made depression my natural state of being and finally caused me to develop post-traumatic stress disorder. Only antidepressants, specialised medication, and invasive treatments were able to eventually resolve the issue and give me hope of having a life again that was not ruled by a temperamental bladder.

The reason I go into such detail is that cystitis is not common in those assigned male at birth, due to the longer urethra, but when it does happen it is devastating for the same reason. Most common in cis-women because of the shorter distance between the opening of the urethra and the bladder, it normally resolves itself within a few days. This compacted anatomy allows the infection to more easily be flushed out. This cannot happen in those assigned male at birth and who have their original biology intact, the twists and turns in the plumbing preventing such escape.

So, when I called up 111 asking for help, they assumed I was female and gave me advice based on that. I was told to drink cranberry juice, take painkillers and wait it out. But it only got worse, and all the while the infection was destroying me from the inside out. When it was finally realised it was an infection that was hanging around and I was given antibiotics, it was too late. The lining of my bladder was shot full of holes and it would be close to a year and several thousand pounds of private treatment before they could fix it again.

So, if you are assigned male at birth and experience something similar, you may need to disclose your gender status to get the appropriate treatment. Better that and an awkward conversation than what I went through.

But what terrified me the most was that such infections would be more common after the operation due to the change in anatomy, and if what had happened to me had caused long-term problems, which the doctors were concerned it would, then the surgery could only make them worse, severely and permanently decreasing my quality of life.

I had to re-evaluate my position on the surgery. Ideally, I wanted to speak to an expert on the matter, perhaps even my surgeon, and while it was requested, it was not possible to arrange on limited notice and with *Covid* still hanging around. Therefore, I needed to make a decision on my own, one that would change the face of my transition, and my life, and perhaps go against what I had always assumed would happen those years ago when I first started contemplating all of this.

What did I do? Just as I had done when picking my university or wondering whether I should jump off my flat's balcony, I made a list of pros and cons. A lot of the pros of having the surgery were to deal with the physical dysphoria, to feel more secure in my body image, not having to worry so much about going outside, to wear what I wanted to wear, as well as to have sex more easily. Whereas the cons were mostly about the pain the surgery would cause, the emotional toll, the risk of complications, the lifelong maintenance I would have to do and the fact that no matter how well the surgery went it would only ever be an approximation. And now I threw the consequences of this infection and the possibility of future infections into the mix.

I asked myself the question. Did I need the surgery?

When I first drew up this list, it was February 2020. Needless to say that a lot had happened since then. Even then the two sides had been fairly equal. Now both were bustling for the lead and it was hard to know for sure without speaking to someone who knew more about this than I did. I also had not yet had all the diagnostic tests so was running along with an incomplete set of data. Nevertheless, the fact they were now so close made me doubt surgery was for me.

I spoke earlier about how the lockdown removed social pressures, and the social gaze, and gave me time to live with my body and image without them. In a way, I got used to them. It was for that reason I had been able to go without make-up for all but special occasions, and in a similar way, it lessened the need to have the surgery to fit some external expectation. I was content with the ninety-five percent completion I had reached and was increasingly unsure if the risks and potential side effects of the surgery were worth crossing that final divide. In an ideal world where everything went perfectly, I would do it without question, but we do not live in that world, so I had to compromise.

I was happy enough. I could live day-to-day without my biology getting in the way. I could manufacture my wardrobe and wear the clothes I wanted and look good doing it. I could wear nice dresses, skirts and tight jeans. I could wear all the things that made me feel and look feminine and not have to worry. And the part it played in sex was becoming less important as time went on.

I was in two polyamorous relationships at the time and have been in more since, becoming increasingly sexually active when my libido started to return around the dawn of 2020, and none could have cared less. They just wanted what made me happy. The sex was good regardless. I enjoyed it. They enjoyed it. If anything, most of them preferred me the way I was. I felt comfortable with who I was and what I could do.

I asked myself the question...

I spoke through it with one of my partners at the time, having one of our late-night heart-to-heart chats that drift through all sorts of vulnerable truths and philosophical musings, and they said something that resonated with me. They did not want to factor into my decision in any way. They wanted me to make the choice that would be best for me, not what I thought other people would want. That stuck with me. It made me go back to my list of pros and cons and see how many of them were for me and how many were for how I would feel being perceived by some amorphous, unidentified third-person perspective. How much of my desire for the surgery came from an inherent need and how much came from a want for acceptance by the 'other'? How much was to fit some stereotype they had established for me? Looking at it, a lot of the cons were things that I could feel. Pain. Direct and unfiltered. Meanwhile, many of the pros were for that outward expectation rather than my own benefit.

My dysphoria was lessening and when I did think about it, it was because of social pressures rather than my own inherent dissatisfaction with my body. The clothes I would want to wear would be for the benefit of the viewer more than my own thrill – a thrill I got with the clothes I already owned. The comfort in sex could be undermined by complications or the lifelong need to dilate, perhaps risking what was good in itself as it was. I liked my body and, as I had found, others did too.

There was an ideal out there, but for now, I could live simpler dreams. I could enjoy time with a partner, wear a nice dress to dinner, and walk down the street without a care in the world. I could have my 'one day' even without the surgery. And that was when I realised that I had lived that 'one day' already. In fact, I had lived several without even noticing it. What more did I need?

And here I had instead experienced a prelude, an echo of the agony that could happen, and I did not want to experience it ever again in any shape or form. And I did not want to lose the dreams I had found reaching for an ideal that may not now be possible, assuming it was ever anything more than a social trick, a gendered aspiration conjured for me to chase, an unattainable perfection to keep me along binary lines, always wanting and waiting for more.

So I asked myself...

It took me time to reach an answer. I did not have all the information I needed. I wanted to speak to someone smarter than myself, and understand the effects of my recent infection and how it all might impact my life post-operation. Until then I had to think on it some more, and who knew... I might find some epiphany along the way.

But with the infection receding and the future once again opening itself to my battered body, broken heart, and shattered soul, I knew that for all that I had suffered, I was going to be okay. Despite everything, and just as I was, I could be happy in health and heart.

And perhaps that was enough.

Chapter Four

The Finish Line

Somehow we make the best of things, even when they go wrong or the plan falls apart, and I had certainly been tasked with that necessity.

Ever since I started the transition, I was convinced that I would need several surgeries to reach a place where I was happy and without dysphoria. But now, after eight years, I found myself in a position where I was going to have none at all. Oddly, that felt okay. The future I had wanted for so long was obliterated by a cruel twist of fate, but even as the knife skewered and spiralled into my heart and mind, the place where it left me was one of resolution. A resolution for what I did not know I had needed.

For three separate reasons, I decided against doing the surgery and, in a single e-mail, undid years of administrative stress and long-held dreams. They unravelled beneath my fingers but in the same breath unveiled the future in a way that made me eager for what was to come.

The best way for me to talk about the 'why' of it all is to list those three reasons separately and give them each their due. The first is related to the medical issues I outlined earlier, the second is to do with the change caused by the lockdown, and the third is a more personal account.

One.

Gender reassignment surgery is invasive and irreversible, one that impacts the body in a large and long-term way. There are several weeks of intense recovery directly afterwards, months of agonised adjustment and then a lifelong adherence to a maintenance routine, and all this for a variable result that could come with its own raft of complications. The pros had only just won out during my first session of self-examination.

But the change in my medical situation knocked my confidence a lot. From the research I did, I understood that it was possible the surgery would cause an increase in the number of similar infections, and possibly longer-term, unforeseen complications. These gave me pause and caused the cons to win out, convincing me that with things as they were, the surgery may not have been in my best interest or benefit my health and mental dysphoria enough to justify the pain it would cause and the possible risks.

Two.

The years of lockdown were a unique and challenging time for many, and while for me they did have their obstacles, one benefit I did not expect was to live with my body and image away from social pressures and expectations. Over quarantine, I spent a lot of time with my body as it was, away from the presentations of everyday life. In doing so, I became used to it and comfortable with its raw appearance. Talking it through with my friends, family and partner, I came to realise that my dysphoria was linked less with my own self-image and self-worth and more with what I thought others expected and wanted from me. I spent so many years of my adolescence living for others, finding acceptance and validation in being what others wanted me to be, that I was carrying it over to this. I would find settlement in pleasing the amorphous 'other' even if it caused me pain and risked my health.

But having found a friendship group and partners that accepted and liked me for who I was, I did not want to cause myself any more trauma by moulding into what I thought others would want. Why apply a binary solution to what was not a binary problem? Why could I not just be me if I was happy? Why must I feel pressured into performing right down to the skin? I had spent too much of my life already living for others. I wanted to finally live for myself. My life, as me, right now, content and forever.

Three.

The transition was a large portion of my life. As I write these words, I am eight years after coming out socially, seven since seeking a referral, six since changing my name, and four since starting hormones. Each step was met by some form of challenge or obstacle to overcome, be it administrative, medical, social, or familial. Each one was a hardship in its own way that caused me stress, frustration, and no shortage of pain and suffering, and the surgery was sure to come with its own raft of traumas and a long period spent in recovery. I suppose that, after all this time, especially after what lockdown and my bladder together put me through, I did not want to think about this anymore. I wanted it to be over. I wanted to be done.

I did not want to be worrying about the next appointment. I did not want to be thinking about the next challenge I would have to meet. I did not want to spend months battling towards and simultaneously fearing the next thing that would cause me pain. I could live everyday life in the way I wanted and had wanted for years. I could present and exist without fear. For those for whom my having the surgery might matter, for those who would even become that intimate, they could not care less. They wanted me to be happy and enjoyed their time with me regardless. And after eight years, I just wanted to get on and finally live. I wanted to spend time enjoying what I had worked so hard to reach. I wanted to spend nights out wearing what I wanted. I wanted to go out for dinner dates with a nice dress on. I wanted to go a day without any more thought for the future than what good it might hold for me. I would rather that than exist in the seemingly endless limbo of the transition, a liminal state, forever unfinished, striving forwards with equal amounts of dread and desperation.

But not anymore.

Because I had been living like that already. I had found my days and lived them well. And all I had to do was accept that I had finished.

Without the surgery looming over me I was free to move on and enjoy the years ahead, live beyond the terror of my infection and the prospect of the surgery and exist as just me.

What I had hoped would come from this finale to my book would no longer be the case, but in a way, it serves to say that you do not need to do anything more than what makes you happy.

Gender is a spectrum and you do not have to mould yourself to fit any singular binary image just because that is what you think others want from you or to believe yourself valid as a transgender person. If you find a place somewhere in between, somewhere that works for you, that makes you happy, then why hurt yourself to go further? You are you, and you are valid wherever you end up. Just live as you and live it well. I can finally see my own finish line after eight years of searching. I truly hope that you, whoever you are, whether you are transgender or not, find your own and can live there for as long as you want.

And so, we come now to the end of my transition in the strict sense as a period of change. I did plan to have an epilogue to this book, but how can I, in a few words, summarise these years of small, subtle moments, many of which have been forgotten when compared to the whole? How can I create a coda to a life that is still ongoing? How can I encapsulate all the lessons that I am still learning? How can I say all that needs to be said without saying everything all over again? Instead, I will not even try because a far better writer has already done it for me. The single most important reason I went through this transition was to become the person I wanted to be and to have that person interact with life and the world at large.

And I succeeded.

For those who have read this far, thank you. Whether you are transgender, know someone who is, or just wanted to learn, it is my wish that you have taken something from these pages. Be it to understand more about yourself, your journey, about a loved one, or about this mad mess of a world and the people that call home, I hope you use it to make it that tiny bit better. For you. For others. For everyone else, now and forever.

'For the growing good of the world is partly dependent on unhistoric acts; and that things are not so ill with you and me as they might have been, is half owing to the number who lived faithfully a hidden life, and rest in unvisited tombs'.[1]

This is not the ending I had envisioned, but it is the one I have reached. So, after nearly a decade, I can at last bow and take my leave.

Farewell.

---

[1] Closing lines of *Middlemarch* by George Eliot.

Appendix

Everyday Interrogations

Living as a member of the LGBT+ community means exposing yourself to discrimination, both subtle and explicit, and the constant questioning of society and the world at large. Most of this is not borne of malice or hatred but simple unfamiliarity.

Little is taught to children in school when it would have the best results, and we are not represented in media nearly enough to make it commonplace. When we are, either the entire story revolves around it or we are often depicted by someone unacquainted with the subject and thus can include misinformation.

These are some of the reasons why I have decided to write my story and my experiences, to present an interior eye into what it is like to live as a transgender woman in today's world. But I am only a single person and can present only a single viewpoint. The truth is that there are as many unique stories as there are people going through the transition. While I cannot represent them all here with any amount of certainty, I can hopefully do so tangentially by answering the most common questions people have about the transition and the community at large. And while some of the questions may appear unnecessarily intrusive or deal with private matters, I would prefer those who are curious to look here rather than force a transgender person to answer questions that may be intensely personal and distressing for them.

These will not be dictionary definition answers and instead come from opinions and experiences formed after years of living as a transgender woman, existing within the community and speaking regularly in interviews, seminars and to curious strangers and acquaintances. Coupled with the main narrative, this should cover the broad strokes shared among the community so that regardless of who you are, you can enter into the discussion with the knowledge needed to be caring and supportive.

What are the different pronouns and why are they important?

The most common pronouns are he/him/his, she/her/hers and they/them/theirs. There are also combinations, such as he/they or she/they. These are the pronouns by which people would prefer to be referred. They are important because by using someone's desired pronouns you are signalling to them that you accept who they are and that you have taken care to welcome them as they would like to be welcomed.

What happens if I deadname or misgender somebody without meaning to do so?

If you are talking to a transgender person and make an honest mistake, either because it is a slip of the tongue or the change has been fairly recent, the important thing is to not make a big fuss about it. Do not beg for forgiveness and most of all do not make the person feel guilty for putting you in this situation. Simply apologise, correct yourself, and move on with the conversation as normal.

If you are talking about a transgender person but they are not present, do your best to catch and correct yourself regardless. This alerts others who may be with you that this person's name or pronouns may be different from what they expect and that it is important to get it right.

A transgender person may not always call you out on it if you get their name or pronouns wrong as it can be awkward to do so, as though they are putting you in an inconvenient position. For this reason, it is good practice to correct yourself if you can and to not assume the gender and pronouns of someone based solely on their appearance. If you are in any doubt, feel free to ask and they will say how they prefer to be called and will be glad that you made the conscientious effort to consider their preference.

What should I do if I am deadnamed, misgendered or challenged about being in a typically gendered space, such as a bathroom or changing room?

If you are deadnamed or misgendered and it was an accident, you are within your right to stop the conversation, calmly state what your preferred name or pronouns are and have the other person correct themselves so you can both move on together.

If it was done maliciously, however, then you are unlikely to change their behaviour. In this case, it is best to extricate yourself from the situation as soon and as politely as you can, to not inspire any further discrimination. Such people and their short-sightedness do not define you. While it may be distressing to have someone poke holes in your identity, it is important to remain true to who you are. It is not that you are not accepted but that they are intentionally limiting their perception to maintain their worldview.

If you are within a public space, highlight your right to be in that space, but if they continue to resist and you are unable to get away, you can attract help from anyone or from a staff member. This does not need to be a cry for help, but simply drawing attention to your situation can be enough to diffuse it and allow you to escape.

If there is no one within sight, there is normally quick access to the emergency services from your phone you can use to attract attention. For example, on the iPhone, press and hold the side button and either volume button until the emergency countdown begins. You can also swipe right on the emergency switch to activate the call immediately. You can also set up emergency features from the settings menu.

If you are accosted by a member of staff, such as in a clothes shop, ask to speak to their manager to point out the discrimination so disciplinary action can be taken. If the manager enforces the resistance, leave and take your custom elsewhere. As it is a commercial faux pas to act against such social causes, offering a poor review online indicating their behaviour can be damaging to their reputation and perhaps cause that business to rethink their policy. Though this need only be done if you feel up to doing so.

What bathroom should a transgender person use and what should I do if I encounter one?

A transgender person can use the facility that matches their gender identity. Some places offer gender-neutral toilets, either as individual rooms or with two facilities that are differentiated only by the presence of urinals in one and not the other. Otherwise, you are free to use either.

It is a common fear that predators will identify as female to gain access to the women's toilets and use that to prey on victims. This is an angle many cis women use in arguments to prohibit transgender women from using the same facilities. In fact, transgender people are far more likely to be on the receiving end of abuse for using the toilet that matches their gender identity than the other way around.

If you encounter someone in the toilets that you believe is transgender and they are simply going about their business, leave them to it. They are responding to the call of nature like everybody else. There is no need to make a scene or cause emotional distress for no valid reason.

How can I introduce my children to gender identity and sexual orientation?

I currently do not have children and am unlikely to in the near future, if at all. Nonetheless, I have given this question a lot of thought. The best way for children to learn about these facets of life would be through their school's sex education class, with a curriculum approved and designed to teach it to them.

This would expose it to them at the right time, in a safe environment, normalise its content and perhaps dissuade the bullying some experience for being outside the assumed 'normal'. However, the system is not set up this way at the moment, so it usually falls on parents to have this discussion with their children.

I believe the fear over this subject comes from the worry that the child, once exposed to these ideas, will want to explore them and come to identify with them. That is a possibility but it is by no means the default. And we may be concerned that we are imparting to them ideas that to us were long considered taboo. However, we must accept that to a child everything is equally new and interesting. What is to us mundane is just as unprecedented and fascinating to them as something that to us is new and long-held as abnormal.

If taught to a child early, the notions of gender and sexual orientation will become part of their held worldview, something that forms the normal part of life and the people within it. You need not go into all the graphic detail regarding these topics, as I have in this book, but enough to let them know that there is more than the binary and it is okay to be attracted to someone who is not necessarily of the 'approved' opposite gender.

You can also look to TV, video games, and media for help in this matter. LGBT+ representation is becoming greater every year and more accessible to people of all age groups. During the course of writing this book, I was watching a show on *Netflix* called *She-Ra: Princess of*

Power. This is an animated show aimed at children but has openly LGBT+ characters in the main cast, and even a transgender side character in one of the later seasons performed by a transgender actor.

Such media can help focus any conversation, be an icebreaker in the discussion and normalise the idea that living this way is accepted, that you can still love and be loved.

My child wants to transition. How can they be sure when they are so young, and is it too early to start considering such a life-altering process?

When they come out, that is not the first step of the process. There will usually have been several months, perhaps even years, of doubt, thought, discomfort and self-examination before they even get the courage to vocalise what they are feeling. Nobody will know how they feel or what they are thinking better than they will. It is worth listening to what they have to say and heeding what this might mean because if they have spoken it out loud it is something serious to them and they trust and love you enough to confide in you and seek your support.

As to whether it is too early, children can be surprisingly astute in matters of the heart, but this is not a decision that is yours to make. It is one to be taken between the child and an expert.

It is therefore wise to explore the channels through which your child could receive help and speak to those who best understand gender dysphoria. They can then advise on the appropriate course of action and liaise with you so you can all move forward together. It is also a possibility that after speaking to an expert, they may gain a greater insight into their feelings and decide they do not want to transition but instead find another outlet through which to express themselves.

Something else to note is that the sooner you get into the process, the better the ultimate results will be, due to puberty blockers preventing their assigned puberty from causing certain irreversible changes to their body that neither hormones nor surgery can fix. Blockers themselves are reversible, and if the transition is ultimately not what they want, these can be stopped and their assigned puberty commence.

My child has come out. How can I tell the rest of the family and what can I do to help, both emotionally and practically?

Some families may find this more difficult due to the individual personalities or beliefs of its members. As such, there is no single rule or guide to follow, but I would recommend speaking with your child so you can figure it out together. You may be surprised at how well some can take the news.

Your child may wish for you to speak to them on their behalf, or they may wish to do it themselves. This can be either to lessen the burden on them so they do not have to come out all over again, in the first case, or to have a greater sense of control over who knows and how in the latter.

When it comes to helping your child through the transition, the most important thing you can do is to love and support them. Be there when they need you and respect their new name, pronouns and gender to the best of your ability. You may also wish to help with more practical matters. Being with them at appointments will matter a lot to them as not every parent has that strength, and helping them with make-up, advice on shaving, or clothes shopping can provide them with crucial information and bonding experiences so you can start to reconnect as a family.

This will not be easy at first as there is a mourning period where you have lost the child you thought you were going to have, but afterwards, you get to discover the child you have now and, to an extent, have always had but who was just hidden away.

Will my child be happy and safe, and did anything influence their decision to take this path?

Happiness is almost always guaranteed for someone going through the transition, as I have hopefully done my best to illustrate throughout the full course of this book. There are hardships and obstacles to overcome, but becoming a fully realised person, and living as who you want to be and the gender you desire is like no other feeling and makes life worth living to its utmost.

Safety, however, is less certain. We still live in a world where discrimination exists and hate crimes are more prevalent against those that identify as LGBT+. I know it is every parent's wish to protect their child, but there is no way to completely guarantee their safety. Supporting them and providing help and love when they need it, however, can enable them to endure the rough moments, and a network of friends and allies, if they live away from home, can perform a similar function. And having the backing of the GIC can provide the necessary weight so that employers and colleagues do not present any issues due to fear of legal repercussions.

You may then think it best for them not to transition, but that does not mean they are safe either. People who are restricted from the transition and the medical treatment and support they need are more likely to experience mental health issues, such as depression, self-harm, and suicidal ideation.

There is no easy path to take and no guarantees, as with most things in life, but you can ensure that they are happy and loved for the path they do decide to take. Because this is their decision and one they believe is best for them.

Do not restrict them or deny them access to information for fear that it will sway them towards one road over another. It is likely that nothing directly influenced their decision in this matter, but instead that they were made aware of the feelings that were always present but until then were unseen and without a name.

For myself, it all happened rather quickly and I cannot pinpoint the exact moment when the lightning bolt struck, but it was only after being exposed to other transgender people that the process truly started. Learning that gender dysphoria existed, how it felt and what the transition was made me look back at my own life and put into place the years I had felt feeling like an outcast and silently envious of the girls around me at school. It made everything make sense in retrospect.

So, while hearing about transgender people and gender identity as a whole will not be something that lures people into transition who do not experience dysphoria, it will allow those who have been feeling like something is wrong with the vocabulary to articulate their problems and the avenues through which to seek a solution.

Am I expected to instantly adjust to their new gender?

The transition is something that happens not only to the individual but to the people around them. While your child may want you to adjust straight away and start using their new name and gender, this will be difficult due to the grief I outlined earlier. However, as long as you are supportive, continue to love them and make the effort to adjust in time, they will understand and wait while you make your own transition.

For my family, it took years for this to happen, and while they might have said the wrong things at times, I never held it against them. I was patient and waited for them to come around so we could be a family again. Because that is what your child will want in the end, to live a normal life and to be part of their family as the person they know themselves to be.

How much does the transition cost and how long does it take?

This depends on where and how you are undertaking the transition. Some countries offer more healthcare than others. I will base my answer on the UK's system as that is the one with which I am most familiar.

The time to go through the most common and affecting stages of the transition can take anywhere from three to ten years and cost between £3,000 to £30,000 based upon whether you are going through the NHS or the private sector.

Most transitions will fall within this range, but exceptional circumstances, such as travelling abroad to receive treatment from an internationally renowned surgeon, for example, can add more to the total cost.

Do you need to have surgery to be considered transgender?

No. Having surgery does not make you any more or less valid as a transgender person. Many people go through the transition but opt not to have any surgery for personal or medical reasons and continue to live as their chosen gender without it. Similarly, you do not need to have started any hormone treatment to be considered transgender. The identity is a self-declaration that comes at a time of your choosing, whenever you are ready.

If you are transgender, do you need to present as either male or female?

No. There is no restriction to the gender as which you present. If you are a transgender woman, for example, you can present in a more feminine manner, a more masculine manner, or somewhere in between.

You may often hear the term 'passing', which refers to a transgender person's ability to present as their chosen gender and conform to its social norms, almost hiding themselves away in the typical cis image. Some do this naturally, some do it to avoid discrimination, while others do it because that is how they wish to present themselves.

Just as with the surgery, being able to 'pass' does not make you any more or less valid, any more or less transgender. Present how you wish and let society catch up to you.

What is the difference between gender identity and sexual orientation and how do the two work together?

Gender identity and sexual orientation are two different aspects of a person's identity that can often be confused due to the overlap of gender in the discussion. Gender identity is a person's internal perception of their gender, whereas sexual orientation is the gender to which that person is attracted when seeking a partner or partners.

If a transgender woman is attracted to other people who also identify as female, that person may identify themselves as a lesbian. Similarly, a transgender man who is attracted to other people who identify as male, that person may consider themselves gay. There are multiple combinations, with each being just as valid as the other, but it is important to remember that gender identity and sexual orientation are separate and can both fluctuate over time.

What is the difference between someone undergoing the transition and someone performing in drag?

I am a transgender woman. When I was born, I was assigned the male gender, but over my life, I came to realise that I was, beneath all this, a woman. I have gone through this transition to represent that, and therefore myself, to the world. In doing so, I dress in ways that appear more feminine, but I can also dress in ways that appear androgynous or fall outside the stereotypical female image. This can also be true of cis women. Some transgender women love dresses and make-up, while others do not. For me, it depends on the situation, but much of the time I go without make-up and dress in casual feminine garb as that, I believe, represents me most adequately and allows me to interact with the world with as few barriers as possible.

The important thing to note is that being transgender is not a performance or someone acting as a character. While it may feel like it at times, I am not on stage playing a part. I am a woman down to my core. This is my identity, through and through.

Drag, on the other hand, is a style of performance. It uses exaggerated feminine or masculine characteristics as part of that performance to create a separate character or persona from the performer themselves, often accompanied by a new name. This can be for a stage show or simply for a fun night out.

Rather than an expression of their true gender, drag is a costume used to perform a character whose gender expression is typically different from that of the performer's usual gender identity. Historically, drag is most commonly performed by cis men that can be either gay or straight. These men may call themselves drag queens. Similarly, drag can also be done by typically cis women as part of a performance or routine, either alone or as part of a group. They can also be gay or straight and may call themselves drag kings.

Transgender people face significant challenges when seeking and occupying employment, as I have described earlier in this book. For that reason, a transgender person may perform in drag as their job because it is something they can do and will be in an accepting environment for them to express who they are. Transgender women who perform in drag often refer to themselves as showgirls, to distinguish themselves from their cis male counterparts who may also perform in drag.

I have often felt uncomfortable around drag queens and have never properly understood why until researching the answer to this question. I have been to several drag shows and was terrified of being picked out by the performer, who could think I was there in drag rather than simply presenting as female for my gender identity. Having thought about it a great deal, I believe I feel this way because being thought of as a drag queen implies that I am not actually a woman and my gender expression is simply a character, that I am playing a part or pretending to be a woman.

What is the difference between being transgender and intersex?

There is sometimes confusion about what it is to be transgender and intersex. When someone is born, their gender is typically assigned based on their sex organs or genitals. For example, when I was born, I had a penis and testicles, so I was assigned the gender 'male'. But for someone who is born without sex organs or genes that fall within the standard definitions of male and female, they are called intersex. For example, some people are born with XY chromosomes (typically male) but have been born with a vagina. Others might have XX chromosomes (typically female) but no uterus, or might have an external anatomy that appears neither male nor female.

Where possible, some intersex people have their gender assigned by force at birth by their parents through surgical intervention. Otherwise, gender can be applied through nurtured social pressures. Many intersex people with XY chromosomes (typically male) but female anatomy are therefore declared female at birth. They are then raised and identified as female, with all the social trappings that come with that identity when one is a child. Many such intersex people and their families may not become aware that their chromosomes are different to their external biology until much later in life.

Being transgender, on the other hand, is determined by one's own internal knowledge of their gender identity. A transgender person is typically born with a body and sex organs that match the standard definitions of 'male' or 'female'. However, as they grow up, they come to realise that their gender identity does not match the gender they were assigned at birth. This identity can fall anywhere within the gender spectrum, including male, female, non-binary, agender, and more.

It is entirely possible for someone to be both transgender and intersex; however, most transgender people are not usually intersex, and similarly, most intersex people are not transgender. For those that are intersex or come to discover later in life that they are intersex, their assigned gender may not fit with their internal sense of gender identity. Therefore, they can make similar changes to their name, appearance, pronouns and social role that many transgender people undertake to start living as the gender that better matches who they are.

What is the difference between being transgender and gender non-conforming?

We live in a binary and gendered world. Therefore, many aspects of our appearance and lifestyle, such as our clothes, hairstyle, speech patterns or hobbies fall within the binary definitions of what is considered 'feminine' or 'masculine'. Those people who choose to present themselves outside these standard extremes because it more accurately represents their identity are known as gender non-conforming.

They may or may not be transgender. The two are not mutually exclusive. Some cis women are raised and identify as women but can present themselves in a way that may be considered more masculine, which can mean they play sports more commonly associated with cis men, dress in masculine clothing and have more masculine speech patterns or demeanours.

Similarly, transgender people may or may not conform to the gender stereotypes for the gender as which they live and identify. They may switch from one to the other or simply dress and act in a way that best represents them.

As a transgender woman, I alter how much I conform to my desired gender depending on the situation. I can dress very feminine or I can dress more masculine. I do this occasionally, wearing jeans and leather jackets with my hair cut short, and forgoing any jewellery or make-up. Or I can wear a cocktail dress with my make-up on and jewels sparkling in the candlelight. It depends on my mood and the occasion. I may conform. I may not. It does not matter either way.

What does it mean to have a gender that is neither male nor female?

Most transgender people identify as either male or female, and they should be treated and accepted as would any other man or woman, but some do not feel that they fit into these binary categories. Some people have a gender that blends aspects of both, one that falls outside either completely or does not identify with any gender at all, and some find that their gender fluctuates over time.

There are many different terms someone might use to describe their gender and I will not list them all here, but if in doubt ask the person how they best wish to be identified. One term that is commonly used, however, is non-binary. This is used because a person's gender does not fit within the usual binary genders of male and female.

Some of those people that identify as non-binary consider themselves to be transgender, while others do not and simply exist and define themselves as who they are and their own personal identity.

Is it too late for me to come out and start my transition?

The short answer is no, but as one gets older the transition may prove either more difficult or less effective. This is because the longer one has lived as the gender to which they were assigned at birth, the more time that gender has had to define that individual, both biologically, and mentally, and in their lifestyle and social ties. Being now more entrenched, there can be greater resistance to any attempt at change. But that does not mean it is impossible or not worth doing. It is never too late to exist as who you know yourself to be and to live happy and free.

What safeguards are in place to ensure the transition can only be accessed by those that need it?

Due to some of the risks involved, the parts that cannot be undone, the time commitment and the resources it takes, the system has been established with several barriers in place. Whether these are excessive or not is not something on which I am qualified to comment, but I do hope that those in such a position become as informed as possible to determine the best solution and offer it the funding it needs to meet the current demand.

Regardless, these barriers, or safeguards, are there to ensure that only those experiencing gender dysphoria and for whom treatment will benefit will undergo the medical stages of the transition. From my own experience, this involved speaking to my GP twice, an independent psychiatrist and two separate consultants who specialise in gender dysphoria. All this occurred over a period of about three years. Only then did I receive my hormone replacement therapy.

To undergo surgery, you go through two further consultations with a consultant and another with the surgeon themselves, with referral only occurring once approval has been received from each. And at every stage, they demand more stringent proof that you are living as your desired gender, such as through evidence of your name change or paychecks to show that you are in employment as your chosen gender.

It does not feel comforting when the people who are meant to help are constantly challenging you and making you prove the validity of your suffering and presentation, but I at least understand the thought behind the practice.

All that being said, you cannot stumble into this process, and if someone is unsure or questioning, this will determine the best course for that individual. And with waiting lists as long as they are and are likely to be for the foreseeable future, there is plenty of time for self-reflection, to call the process to a halt should you wish it.

It is easier, after all, to drop out than it is to get through the door.

Do transgender people ever regret going through the transition?

Most people who undergo the transition become happier and more secure in their lives as a result, such as I have. However, there can be occasions when someone may regret the path they have taken. This is usually not due to the transition process itself, but the obstacles it presents in the form of problems at work, strained relationships with friends and family, and discrimination out in the world. A small percentage of these may regret the physical changes of the transition as well, but they are the outliers of a widely successful process.

Are any parts of the transition reversible?

There are three main parts to the transition that follow the sections of this book: the social, the hormonal, and the surgical.

Anything done purely socially or administratively is reversible, as names can be changed and people updated if someone decides to revert to presenting and identifying with their birth gender.

For the hormonal part, it depends on which kind of treatment is being done. For those under eighteen, puberty blockers are completely reversible. They only pause the body's natural function, and if removed the body would then proceed as normal. For those over eighteen, hormone replacement therapy has a mixture of reversible and irreversible elements. Sterility, for example, is permanent, but fat distribution is not.

Any surgical measures are mostly irreversible, and those few that are not can only be done at your own expense.

It is for this reason that there are so many checks and consultations a person must undertake before they have access to any medical intervention.

Does being transgender preclude one from having children?

While hormone replacement therapy does cause sterility, this is factored into the process and there are options for gamete storage, be it for sperm or egg cells.

Due to this, a transgender person can have a child through either a partner or a surrogate, depending on their situation. There is also the possibility to adopt should they wish it or if gamete storage is not successful or possible in their case. This is all dependent upon their desire to have children, which can vary from person to person and change over time.

If gender is fluid and can be self-identified then what is the purpose of gender at all?

When digging into the discussion, it can seem that gender, at its core, is arbitrary. In a sense, it is. Gender is a social construct that has been implemented into society due to the biological differences between the two most common sexes. To find acceptance, should it not matter how we identify but that we are nothing more than human?

In an ideal world, perhaps. But that is not the world in which we live. Our society is heavily gendered and binary. It is so ingrained that even before you learn someone's name, cues on appearance, behaviour, lifestyle and even shape can inform you of someone's gender and provide assumptions on how you should interact with them and address them. These assumptions, while they can work for many cases, are not always correct, and it is here that transgender people battle every day.

A core part of being human is to categorise. It is why every species and subspecies on this planet has its own name and minute descriptors that differentiate it from its neighbour. Why then should this tendency not apply to us? As such, we have found words and labels, definitions that describe us beyond these binary assumptions. With them, we can declare our place in the world, communicate who we are and find acceptance. It also helps us come to terms with who we are and how we ourselves fit into it.

I did not know why I felt lost or wrong when I was younger, but when I found the words, I suddenly had a way to define and vocalise what I felt. It gave me power and it gave me place. If you find words that best illustrate who you are, they are your tools for finding your own place in this world, and I will accept you whatever those words might be.

What is meant by conversion therapy and why does it occur?

Conversion therapy is the pseudoscientific practice of through force, coercion, persuasion or inducement convincing someone that they are not LGBT+ and that they should continue to live in the cis and heterosexual way approved and ordained for them.

People are often taken to such institutions against their will, or with outside measures influencing them, and sometimes by their own families.

The 'therapy' itself usually takes the form of attempting to change a person's gender identity or sexual orientation, which they assume to be a form of mental illness, through psychological, physical or spiritual interventions, the latter usually through religious pressures. There have also been stories of abuse and corrective rape being used as methods of conversion.

It perpetuates historic views of gender roles, as well as the negative stereotype that being LGBT+ is abnormal and warrants correcting. Most importantly, it puts young people at risk of serious harm, either at the hands of their 'therapist' or themselves, through depression, anxiety, and suicidal ideation.

Though it is a vile practice, with no evidence to say that it is effective and that someone can even be changed in such a way, many countries still permit it to occur. Some jurisdictions have made laws against it, but in both the UK and the US it is legal, despite governments expressing their concerns and promising to outlaw it.

If I believe someone I see is transgender, what should I do and what questions is it acceptable to ask of a transgender person? Should I ask if they have had any surgeries?

Unless a transgender person explicitly states that they are transgender, there is no need to probe any further. You only need to accept them at face value and how they present themselves. If they do state that they are transgender, the only question you need to ask is what name and pronouns as which they prefer to be referred to. This signals to them your willingness to accept them and to alter your behaviour to accommodate them into the world.

Beyond this, there are no questions you should ask of a transgender person. If they feel confident enough to discuss more aspects of their life, they will do so at their own pace. Do not try to force answers from them as this will erode any trust you might have built and make them less likely to confide in you as a friend.

The only time in which it is acceptable to have a conversation about whether a transgender person has had any surgery is if you are in a relationship with them and are considering making it sexual. In this case, allow them to begin and lead the discussion when they are willing to do so. This allows you to both be on the same page regarding what to expect, what to do, how to make each other comfortable, what you would each prefer to do and what actions and parts of the body should be avoided.

Be prepared that if you do something they do not like, either before or during the act, they may withdraw their consent to have sex, in that instant or entirely. If this happens, respect their boundaries and allow them the time and space they need. Sex for a transgender person can be a minefield of confusing feelings, embarrassment, and anxiety. All you need to do is support them and be there for them, not satisfy your own curiosity at their expense.

If you are not in the above situation, then the intimate details of a transgender person's body are as much your business as yours is to them. That is to say, none at all.

With whom do transgender people have sex and how do they have sex?

The people with whom a transgender person has sex or with whom they have a romantic connection are no different to those a cis person would. It is based on their sexual orientation. For example, I am a transgender woman and I consider myself pansexual. I am attracted to people regardless of their gender. It is more about the person and our connection on such a level. Similarly, a transgender man who is attracted to women may consider himself straight or heterosexual.

How transgender people have sex is also no different from cis people. It is based on what sex organs they have, either based upon what they have from birth or what they have attained through surgical means. For example, a transgender woman who has not had any surgeries and who prefers to be a receptive partner would do so using the anus, whereas one who has had their gender reassignment surgery could use either their anus or their newly formed vagina. On the other hand, a transgender woman may also prefer to be the penetrative partner, in which case they could use the penis they may have from birth or could use toys or prosthetics to achieve a similar effect.

There is no single way to have sex. It can be moulded to suit each individual and the person or people they are with to find what is most comfortable and pleasing for all involved. The key is clear communication between partners, so they are all aware of what is happening, what is allowed and what is not. However, such details are personal and matter only to those parties involved. You should not ask a transgender person such questions unless you are in a situation where it would be relevant for you to know, such as if you were planning to have sex or were in a relationship together. Otherwise, it holds as little relevance to you as your sex life would to them.

Why does there seem to be more transgender people now than before? Is being transgender a new thing?

There is evidence of transgender people, those who do not conform to our current ideas of binary gender roles, and members of the LGBT+ community in the historical record, in Victorian and Viking culture, ancient Greece, Rome and Egypt, among others. It has been here for millennia, much to the initial confusion of some historians who viewed history through our modern, binary lens.

However, the world has been strongly patriarchal for almost as long as there has been civilisation, and the modern world has followed this trend. It is one built upon colonial expansion, which spread to the four corners the notions of western patriarchy, social gender roles, and the religious exclusion of anything beyond the union of a man and a woman, and these as the binary genders. Many indigenous cultures at that time had a wider view of gender and sexuality, but they were seen as uncultured and in need of civilising by the colonial powers. Also, a lot of the research, institutions and historical documents around transgender people were destroyed during the 20th century and before, during various censorship campaigns, dictatorships and governments curating their view of history through book burnings, pedagogy, and indoctrination.

This view has only started to crumble in the last half-century or so. For example, in the UK, it was illegal to be homosexual until 1967. Perhaps most famously, Alan

Turing, the mathematician who helped break the German enigma code and shorten World War Two by an estimated two years, was convicted of being gay. To spare himself imprisonment, he chose chemical castration through enforced hormone supplements. In the end, he committed suicide by eating a poisoned apple. Then there were the Stonewall Riots, the AIDS epidemic and Section 28, which prohibited the promotion of homosexuality until 2003, which propagated the social dialogue that anything beyond the heterosexual binary was somehow inherently wrong.

Now, however, being gay is a protected characteristic, enshrined in law as something that cannot be used against someone, and it is also considered social suicide to openly speak out against the community. This is a rapid and sudden shift for the better, but it is new in the relative memory of society. And while the L, G and, to a lesser extent, the B have reached more mainstream awareness, the T is only just starting to make itself known.

For that reason, those people who would have before hidden away in fear and shame, refusing to come out, now feel that it is perhaps safe to do so. Therefore, more transgender people are seeking the help they need to live as the gender as which they identify. Though, this does mean it is putting great strain on a system not designed for such numbers.

For those outside of the community, this relatively new acceptance and the purposeful eradication of much of its place in history makes it appear as a new phenomenon.

In fact, it is a situational and observational bias for what has always been there and a part of what it means to be human.

There are so many new terms, words, sexual orientations and identities. How can I be expected to memorise all of them and use them correctly in everyday conversation?

The language around gender identity and sexual orientation is relatively new and constantly changing. Words that were once slurs, like 'queer', are now akin to a badge of honour, while other words, like 'transexual', have been disinherited by the community due to the connotations it draws between gender and sex. It can seem daunting to keep up to date with this adapting vocabulary, but you do not need to. The only thing you need to remember is to use the words, pronouns, and terms that matter to those people around you, and be conscientious that others may not use the standard array of cis-heterosexual terminology.

If you make the effort to adapt, it will mean more than you know to those people for whom it matters. They will be understanding and patient and will not punish or ridicule you for making a mistake. They might make mistakes as well. I know I have in the past. And if you do misgender them by accident, follow the advice I gave earlier in this section and move on.

Just be kind and respectful, and everything else will follow.

Glossary

The vocabulary around gender identity and sexual orientation is relatively new in the grand scheme of the natural evolution of language over time. Words that were once used as slurs have been reclaimed, while other words that were once definitions have fallen out of favour, while yet more are still being coined. This glossary is not exhaustive and instead acts as a snapshot of the terms used throughout this book and those in common use by the community at the time of writing.

Agender: When someone does not identify with any gender. They may consider themselves gender-neutral, non-binary or simply without a gender identity.

Asexual: When someone does not feel sexual attraction to anyone and has low or non-existent sexual feelings in general.

Assigned Female at Birth (AFAB): The term used to describe a transgender person who was given the birth gender of female but now identifies as a different gender.

Assigned Male at Birth (AMAB): The term used to describe a transgender person who was given the birth gender of male but now identifies as a different gender.

Bisexual: The romantic or sexual attraction to both males, females and those who identify outside these binary definitions.

Cis: Someone for whom their gender identity aligns with the gender they were assigned at birth.

Deadname (Noun): The name a transgender person was given when they were born, but with which they no longer use to identify themselves.

Deadname (Verb): The act of using a transgender person's deadname instead of their chosen name. This can be done maliciously or accidentally, but either way can cause great emotional distress to the person in question.

Gay: Also known as 'homosexual', the romantic or sexual attraction by someone who identifies as male to another person who also identifies as male.

Gender Dysphoria: A feeling of discomfort and pervading unease one feels when their gender identity does not match the gender as which they live.

Gender Euphoria: A feeling of overwhelming contentment and happiness one feels when their gender identity matches the gender in which they live.

Gender Fluid: Gender fluid describes people whose gender identity changes over time. One may identify as a male on a particular day and then female on the next. They may also identify as transgender, agender, or any other non-binary identity.

Gender Reassignment Surgery (GRS): Also known as gender confirmation surgery, this is either one or a set of operations that are used to align a person's external biology to that of their internal gender identity, usually but not exclusively focused on their birth sex organs.

Heterosexual: Also known as 'straight', this is the romantic or sexual attraction by someone to the opposite gender, typically between male and female.

Hormone Replacement Therapy (HRT): A medical process by which a transgender person is given hormone supplements and blockers to adjust the levels in their body, producing physical changes akin to the puberty of their desired gender. For example, for transgender men, this involves their voice breaking and becoming deeper, and for transgender women, their skin becoming softer and breasts growing, among other changes.

Lesbian: The romantic or sexual attraction by someone who identifies as female to another person who also identifies as female.

Non-Binary: Someone whose gender identity does not fit within the binary definitions of male and female. They may consider themselves transgender or they may not.

Misgender: The act of using the incorrect gender terminology or pronouns when referencing a transgender person. This can be done maliciously or accidentally.

Pansexual: An extension of bisexuality, this is the romantic or sexual attraction to someone regardless of their gender or gender identity. As time goes on, the definitions of 'pansexual' and 'bisexual' are becoming more closely aligned, and it is likely that they may become synonyms.

Passing: When a transgender person is able to present as their chosen gender, usually as either male or female, to the extent that they are not told apart from their cis counterparts.

Polyamorous: Also known as 'Ethically Non-Monogamous', this is when someone is in a relationship with more than one partner. These can be independent or all experienced together.

Polycule: The network formed by multiple polyamorous relationships.

Trans man: A transgender person who was assigned female at birth but now identifies as male.

Trans woman: A transgender person who was assigned male at birth but now identifies as female.

Transgender: The term used to describe someone whose gender identity differs from the one they were assigned at birth.

Transition: The method by which transgender people adjust their body, lifestyle, and social connections to present and inhabit the gender as which they identify. This can include medical processes and surgeries, or it may not. There is no single way to transition, only to reach the stage that best suits the individual.

Transvestite: A now outdated term that describes someone who cross-dresses, or who dresses and acts in the style of the gender opposite to the one they were assigned at birth. This is not done as a permanent change, but instead during select occasions. This term has now been folded into the umbrella of 'transgender' or 'gender fluid'.